The

Hustle

Code

The Hustle Code
Copyright © 2017

All rights reserved. This book may not be reproduced in any form, in whole or in part (beyond the copying permitted by U.S. Copyright Law, Section 107, "fair use" in teaching or research, Section 108, certain library copying, or in published media by reviewers in limited excerpts), without written permission from the authors.

This book is licensed for your personal enjoyment only. This book may not be resold without written permission of the publisher. Thank you for respecting the hard work of the authors.

Disclaimer:

Thank you for buying and reading this book. The information in this book can potentially improve the quality of your life and the lives of others. If you find any mistakes, PLEASE tell us by sending the error and page you found it on to our email Info@BookFamous.com We thank you and appreciate your feedback.

While best efforts have been used, the authors are not offering legal, accounting, medical or any professional advice and make no representations or warranties of any kind and assume no liabilities of any kind with respect to the accuracy or completeness of the contents and specifically disclaim any implied warranties of merchantability or fitness of use for a particular purpose, nor shall the authors be held liable or responsible to any person or entity with respect to any loss or incidental or consequential damages caused, or alleged to have been caused, directly or indirectly, by the information or programs contained herein. The views expressed are those of the authors alone, and should not be taken as expert instruction or commands. The reader is responsible for his or her own actions. Adherence to all applicable laws and regulations, including international, federal, state, and local governing professional licensing, business practices, advertising, and all other aspects of doing business in the United States or any other jurisdiction is the sole responsibility of the purchaser or reader. Neither the authors nor the publisher assumes any responsibility or liability whatsoever on the behalf of the purchaser or reader of these materials.
www.BookFamous.com

Table of Contents

Introduction 5

My Recipe For Success In Business, Selling and Life.. 7

From Orphan to CEO 25

Punch Cards 48

Heart of an Underdog 67

Turning Tragedy into Triumph 84

Hard Work Beats Talent 103

Everyone Has Potential, Few Put in the Work 123

From Juvenile Offender to Family Defender.. 136

Adapting to Adversity 151

Smart Hustle 161

INTRODUCTION

The intention of The Hustle Code book project is to inspire other Latinos to think bigger and reach higher than ever before. In this book, we peel back the curtains and share a unique point of view from 10 Latino role models as they write about their humble beginnings and the action they took to get them closer to their personal goals. Every story in this book is unique, yet they are similar in their message about personal challenges. Everyone faces obstacles and these authors are no different. They want to share what they do to get over the daily challenges that life puts in our way to test our will and character. We are now living in the most exciting times for all Latinos as we are growing in numbers and uniting towards a better future for our children despite of what the media wants you to believe. We trust you that will enjoy and most importantly to take action and move towards what is possible. We thank you for your support and look forward to seeing you grow!

MY RECIPE FOR SUCCESS IN BUSINESS, SELLING AND LIFE

MY STORY IS ABOUT PASSION, OBSESSION, PURPOSE, DRIVE, AND DISCIPLINE

For the record, I don't have a degree. I am not a writer. English is my second language, and I have a record. I am one lucky guy... Growing up in Chile, my first eight years of life were way different from what my life is today.

My father went to the United States in search of a better life for our family in 1970. My mother followed in 1972. My brother, Chris, and I came in 1975 and finally my other brothers, Hans and Max (twins), and my sister, Lisbett, came a couple of years after. My father was the one who went back and forth from the United States to Chile to get us.

It took about seven years for all of us to be together as a family again. I remember my father leaving Chile, thinking that I would never see him again, and the pain that I suffered. I felt the same pain or maybe worse when my mother left. More pain and sadness again when Chris and I left, leaving my little siblings and my grandmother (who was taking care of us) behind.

To this day, I have never experienced so much pain and sadness. I remember the trip from Chile to the United States like it was yesterday, although it was forty years ago. I think I cried the entire month it took to arrive in Los Angeles, California. They were some of my saddest days to date.

As I tell my story, I always mention the movie *Planes, Trains and Automobiles*, because that was pretty much how we made it to America… illegally! Not really knowing where I was and running across Interstate 5 in San Diego, like I was running for my life. I had no idea how dangerous what we were doing was. To me it was a game in a way… Who could get to the other side of the freeway the fastest.

As we made it into San Diego, my father said, "We made it." I wasn't too sure, because all the street signs that I was reading were all in Spanish… San Diego, Del Mar, La Jolla, Santa Monica, Los Angeles, etc. I remember being so confused. However, at the same time, you can imagine a little kid with eyes wide open looking at this country with admiration—the cleanliest paved streets and highways, all the lights, and the beautiful houses.

Even the worst parts of the city in Los Angeles were so pretty to me. Coming from Chile, in those times, you have to remember that the houses were old, with sheet metal as roofs, no insulation, no carpet, and at times not even a real floor, just dirt floors or cement.

Once I saw my mother again, all my pain was forgotten. We settled in Van Nuys in a studio apartment, where the four of us lived.

It must have been October, because all of a sudden I remember the doorbell ringing time after time and kids dressed in costumes asking for candy. Again, I was so confused. I didn't know it was Halloween. In Chile, it was not celebrated.

Soon after, we moved into another apartment in Van Nuys… but this time it was much larger—a two bedroom, one bath place. We were so impressed and so happy with our father for making this happen for us.

Not much later, my father went back to Chile to bring Max, Hans, and Lisbett to California, so we could all be reunited once and for all as a family… It was a full house. Seven of us sharing a two-bedroom, one-bathroom apartment. Once again, my father moved us to another house, yes, this time a home.

To me it was a mansion, compared to where I came from. Again, it was located in a Los Angeles suburb city called Van Nuys. It was not the best of neighborhoods, but we didn't care. It was our 900-square foot, three-bedroom, one-bath home. It was here where we ended up until I moved out at 18 years old. But, it was also here where all the troubles started.

At 12 years old, my parents were getting divorced. I had to step up and help out around the house. Soon after, my father went away for over a decade.

> "The only people I have ever known to have no problems are in the cemetery."
> —Norman Vincent Peale

I still remember my mother's eyes, wondering how she was going to raise five kids by herself, not knowing a word of English. She barely knew how to drive, obviously had no college degree, and no work experience. Now what? Sure enough, my mother came up with a plan.

First, my grandmother had to come from Chile to California to take care of us while my mother worked. The plan was to clean two houses a day at $50 each and two disgusting 76 gas station bathrooms at $14 each, twice per week, and I had to help her. YUCK! If you are doing the math, it's $560 per week. In the late 1970s, that wasn't bad at all. It was enough to support a household of seven, with five of us in our teens. You parents reading this book, you know what I am talking about in terms of cash needed to support, feed, and clothe five teenagers, right?

Anyway, I drove my mom around town, cleaning gas station bathrooms (keep in mind I was barely a teen). I did this after school, and I was embarrassed that if I ran into friends, as we were cleaning those filthy gas station bathrooms, what they would say.

Eventually, it just became normal, and I was so proud of my mother for making it happen for us. My mom said she had to do whatever legal job happened to come up. She was a hustler and her confidence and attitude totally changed for the better.

I AM AN AVERAGE PERSON WITH AN ABOVE AVERAGE DESIRE.

I was about 12 years old when I got my first job in a barber shop about 10 miles away. I rode my bicycle to go and sweep the floors for $20. I thought, *WOW! I am making it happen.* LOL!

Then, I moved up to work in a factory, filling shampoo bottles… boring! As I was becoming more and more ambitious, because I got a little taste of having a few bucks, I started reading more about business success. I didn't know it at the time, but I guess I was mentally training my mind for the positive outcomes.

Today, I know I was using a powerful tool called visualization. If you haven't practiced this success technique and want to achieve greatness in your life, whether it be in business, relationships, or selling, I highly recommend you start reading about visualization. It will change your life, as it did mine.

High school came fast, and my school was borderline to Encino, which was a much more affluent part of town. (I lived on the wrong side of the tracks.) I remember my first day of school, watching as rich kids were driven and dropped off in limousines and others were driving their BMWs, Porsches, and Mercedes-Benz. That was the first time I felt jealousy and envious.

Why did they have so much more than I did? However, it was also an eye opener for me. Seeing what was out there in the world, I wanted to go for it. During my years growing up, my father gave me many great things, including a drum set to drive my mom crazy. He also promised me his Porsche, as soon as I turned 16. I was so excited. I couldn't wait for my sixteenth birthday to arrive. I remember bragging to all my friends, letting them know what I was getting for my birthday.

My sixteenth birthday came and went and no car. I never told my father how disappointed I was with him. I have never held a grudge. I just never asked him for anything else, ever again. My poor mother felt so bad that, with the little money she had, she purchased a very used 1978 Volkswagen Rabbit for about one thousand dollars. It needed lots of work, so I had to sell my gorgeous drum set my father gave me to make my car cool to cruise the streets.

I also needed a job. So, I started delivering pizza for a local pizza shop in my neighborhood. A few years later, I sold my VW Rabbit for four thousand dollars. I was in heaven and quickly figured out that if I took care of what I owned, I could sell it for a profit later on.

I then purchased my own car when I was about 17 or 18 years old. It was a deep blue, Mazda RX-7 for four thousand dollars. I sold that car two years later for sixty-five hundred dollars. I barely graduated from high school, and I wanted material things faster than I was getting paid. It was about that time when I started getting in trouble with the law.

I was in and out of jail and, at 21 years old, the judge had enough of me. She sentenced me to a year in jail and five years' probation. Judge Patricia Schwartz also let me know that the next time I was in her courtroom, she would sentence me to a minimum of five years in prison. I was so mad at myself that I had disappointed the people who loved me the most.

From that point forward, I promised myself to never ever do such stupid things. I never did. It was my calling to just better myself.

I went to the local bookstore and purchased just about every self-help book. I attended dozens of seminars on human behavior, psychology, and selling techniques from some of the greatest speakers of all time. Names like Zig Ziglar, Tom Hopkins, Brian Tracy, Tony Robbins, Les Brown, Jim Rohn, Wayne Dyer, Stephen Covey, Jack Canfield, Grant Cardone, Darren Hardy, and so many more. I knew that I had to give it all I had, because I did not have a plan B.

From age 18 to 22, I had about 26 different jobs. They included selling vacuum cleaners door to door, selling pagers, selling insurance, selling water filters, recruiting, selling advertising, telemarketing, and so many more. Until, one day in 1989, I was referred to a custom clothier by a friend.

I sold him a couple of pagers and asked him why he needed two pagers. His reply was that one was for his clothing business and the other was for his real estate investments. I must have made a great impact on him, because he immediately offered me a sales job. Of course, I declined, gambling that he would pursue me for the position, and it worked.

About a month later, I was selling custom suits and shirts direct to the public, which he never thought about doing. Immediately, I was his top sales rep, and he treated me great—Vegas trips, private jet, limousines, expensive dinners, and more. I was hooked and wanted more.

Two years later, we became business partners and opened shop in Encino. Life was great. Until the early 1990s, when the Kuwait recession hit and it hurt everyone, including us. In 1992, I had to file for bankruptcy and find a job. I was recruited by a hair replacement company called Hair Replacement Center (HRC) and within months I was the leading sales representative, bringing in $60,000 plus a month in revenue. In six months, I was running the company with 12 branches as their corporate sales director and doing great. In 1993, I was married. In January 1994, I purchased my first house; however, the hair business was not for me.

> "Most people don't plan to fail; they fail to plan."
> —John L. Beckley

I took another gamble and went back into clothing on 100 percent commission. However, this time I was with the largest custom clothing company in the world. Once again, within two months out of three thousand worldwide sales people, I was number three.

On April 2, 1997, I decided to go for it and do it on my own. I just had this gut feeling that I could and would make it happen, no matter what it took. A year later, we were living the life in this gorgeous dream home behind gates in an affluent Thousand Oaks neighborhood.

I was living the dream, but I wasn't happy. All I was doing was working myself to death, and I thought that life was not supposed to be like that, if I had all this success. I was barely seeing my family and my kids. I was building a business, and I remember saying to myself that it didn't matter what it took to make it happen.

Unfortunately, it was destroying my family and, in 2002, my wife and I filed for divorce. My ex-wife and I met when I was eight or nine years old. She even taught me some English. Today, we are still good friends, and my kids love that.

I ended up living in hotels for a couple of years until I figured out where I wanted to live. One of my dreams was to own a place in Pasadena on South Orange Grove Avenue near the Wrigley Mansion. I purchased a stunning place and quickly found out that the average age of people in that neighborhood was about 80 years old. Needless to say, a few years later, I decided to move to downtown to a cool loft with a much younger, hip crowd.

In late 2007, the economy was collapsing again; my mother was diagnosed with cancer; my business was down 40 percent, I lost about a thousand clients, and I was served with a tax fraud judgment from the Internal Revenue Service (IRS). Not a fun time.

At that time, I didn't care for anything else but for my mother to get well. I remember getting a call from my mother letting me know that she was diagnosed with leukemia cancer. I was on the 101 Freeway around the Hollywood area. I had to pull over. I cried for a few hours, drove to my Los Angeles showroom, and got drunk for three days trying to figure out how this could happen to my mother. I was devastated.

I have never experienced so much pain, and for the first time in my life, I didn't know how to handle it or how to fix it. I went into a depression for about six months and just didn't care. I was losing my cars, my houses, and depleting my savings. One day I just woke up and went back to basics and started pushing, reading, working out, and becoming my enthusiastic, driven, motivated, filled with purpose self again. I didn't enjoy that dark place I had been in.

I had to prove to myself and to my family that I could do it again. The year 2008 was my worst year to date, and I had to change with the times. I started networking, attending seminars again, and social media was booming. I started learning as much I could about social media marketing and became really good at it. I even taught a course on it. I promised myself, that I would never go back to that dark place again.

In 2009, I changed many things about me for the better and just started kicking ass. I was getting interviewed by the *Los Angeles Times,* American Express, CNN TV, *Esquire,* the National Football League (NFL), and so many other media outlets. I was back and coming back stronger than ever.

The purpose of my story is not to brag, but to share that life throws many blows at us. Most people quit and never do anything to overcome the challenges. I came from very humble beginnings and made something of myself.

LET ME SHARE FIVE THINGS THAT OTHER SUCCESSFUL FRIENDS AND I DO BEFORE 8:00 AM...

RISE AND SHINE!

Morning time just became your new best friend. Love it or hate it, utilizing the morning hours before work might be the key to a successful and healthy lifestyle. That's right, early rising is a common trait found in many corporate executive officers (CEOs), government officials, and other influential people. Former British Prime Minister Margaret Thatcher was up every day at 5:00 AM, American architect Frank Lloyd Wright was up at 4:00 AM, and the CEO of the Walt Disney Company, Robert Iger, wakes at 4:30 AM, just to name a few.

I know what you're thinking—you do your best work at night. Not so fast. According to *Inc. Magazine,* morning people have been found to be more proactive and more productive. In addition, the health benefits for those with a life before work go on and on. Let's explore five of the things successful people do before 8:00 AM.

1. Exercise. I've said it once; I'll say it again. Most people who work out daily, work out in the morning. Whether it's a morning yoga session or a trip to the gym, exercising before work gives you a boost of energy for the day and that deserved sense of accomplishment. Anyone can tackle a pile of paperwork after 200 ab reps! Morning workouts also eliminate the possibility of flaking out on your cardio after a long day at work. Even if you aren't bright eyed and bushy tailed at the thought of a 5:00 AM jog, try waking up 15 minutes early for a quick bedside set of pushups or stretching. It'll help wake your body and prep you for your day.

2. Map Out Your Day. Maximize your potential by mapping out your schedule for the day, in addition to your goals and to-do lists. The morning is a good time for this, as it is often one of the only quiet times a person gets throughout the day. The early hours foster easier reflection that helps when prioritizing your activities. They also allow for uninterrupted problem solving, when trying to fit everything into your timetable. While scheduling, don't forget about your mental health. Plan a 10-minute break after that stressful meeting, perhaps a quick walk around the block or a moment of meditation at your desk. Trying to eat healthy? Schedule a small window in the evening to pack a few nutritious snacks to take to work the next day.

3. Eat a Healthy Breakfast. We all know that rush out the door with a cup of coffee and an empty stomach feeling. You sit down at your desk, and you're already wondering how early that taco truck sets up camp outside your office. No good. Take that extra time in the morning to fuel your body for the tasks ahead of it. It will help keep your mind on what's at hand and not your growling stomach. Not only is breakfast good for your physical health, it is also a good time to connect socially. Even five minutes of talking with your kids or spouse while eating a quick bowl of oatmeal can boost your spirits before heading out the door.

4. Visualization. These days, we talk about our physical health ad nauseam, but sometimes our mental health gets overlooked. The morning is the perfect time to spend some quiet time inside your mind, meditating or visualizing. Take a moment to visualize your day ahead, focusing on the successes you will have. Even just a minute of visualization and positive thinking can help improve your mood and outlook on your workload for the day.

5. Make Your Day Top Heavy. We all have that one item on our to-do list that we dread. It looms over you all day (or week) until you finally suck it up and do it, after much procrastination. Here's an easy tip to save yourself the stress—do that least desirable task on your list first. Instead of anticipating the unpleasantness of it from first coffee through your lunch break, get it out of the way. The morning is the time when you are (generally) better rested and your energy level is up. Therefore, you are better equipped to handle more difficult projects. And look at it this way, your day will get progressively *easier*, not the other way around. By the time your work day is ending, you're winding down with easier to dos and heading into your free time more relaxed. Success!

My purpose is to make you think about your **dreams**—because I am pretty sure if you are reading this book, you are a dreamer, just like me.

You see the greatest tragedy in life is not death… but living your life bound by dramatic experiences from your past. I've learned that success comes after you have pay the price. I've also learned that success leaves clues and that all successful people have roadmaps.

**"The secret of getting ahead is getting started."
—Mark Twain**

You're a grown-up… there comes a point in time, where you have to take control of your own life.

- Wherever you're from
- Whoever did you wrong
- If you are from a broken family
- Poor or rich
- No money or bankruptcy
- Divorced
- Mentally or physically abused

We all have at least one of these in our past… I just choose not to dwell on them. Someone else's opinion of you does not have to become your reality.

Don't let others control your destiny.

When I first started in sales, my family and my friends thought I was crazy going to work for free (on commission). Now, I tell them working for free made me rich, biatch… LOL!

My mother believed in me. When I used to come home from a long day out in the field, my mother always asked, "How was your day?"

I said, "Mom, my day was fantastic, but no sales."

She always said, "Not to worry, son; tomorrow will be a better day."

So, this was my **drive** to prove to everybody that I could do this.

It became my **obsession.**

I ask you… Why not use the two most important words in the world?

So, you want to hear what these words are? **What if?**

Every single question starts with what if?

Change is instant, when you're ready. Are you ready?

My success wasn't overnight, but then again what is, unless you win the lottery? My point is to always keep hungry, motivated, have a great desire to achieve, and have a mental mindset to be the best. Greed is not good, passion is what is good. Don't settle for average—you are better than that. Have vision, have courage, have clarity, have purpose, have drive, have love, and you must have conviction.

> *"In my walks, every man I meet is my superior in some way, and in that I learn from him."*
>
> —Ralph Waldo Emerson

ACKNOWLEDGMENTS

To my parents, my mother for teaching me perseverance and always letting me know that **I can do it!** Te amo Mami. To my father for teaching me discipline and teaching me I am the best at whatever I do. **Do it right or don't do it at all**. Gracias, Papi. Thank you for the gift of my adventurous life.

To my kids, Alexis, Amanda, and little Art. Thank you for always being there for me, even when there were times I couldn't be there for you. I love you so much.

To my countless mentors responsible for my real-world education, eye-opening scenarios through my years of this life. To name a few, Perkash Vaswani, Craig Tshudi, Ray Montalvo, Judge Patricia Schwartz, Michael Papale, Daniel Simons, and Jack Taylor.

To my special friends and family through my life journey who put up with all my ramblings about life, relationships, salesmanship, business, and so much more. Michael Papale, Alex Diaz, Lisa Medina, Hector Rendon, Doug Carlton, Scott and David Cacurak, Richard Taylor, Edwin Tuazon, Jerry Bakhchyan, Barry Fischer, Martin Cuevas, Hans Lewin, Max Lewin, Christian Lewin, Lisbett Lewin, Mama Irma, Tia Sylvia, Tia Eli, Tio Carlos, Andrea Lewin, Ericka Lewin, Alisha Lewin, Mia Lewin, Tio Toto, Mama Martha, Donnie Gasaway, Karen Gasaway, Denise Andeson, Ben and Nichole Hoss, Sarah Baktiahr, Ricardo Abrines, Bob Donnell, Dr. Andrew Thorn, Evan Cole, Thomas Elliott, Chris Limon, Joe Vivanco, David Vivanco, John Raygoza, Craig Thomas, Michael Saltman, Paul Frias, Greg Pyle, Rex Maningding, Rande & Rosemarie Ferguson, Rune Eriksson, Steven Roth, Tom Jackels, Todd Maxwell, Olman Valverde, Saul Aguilar, Freddy Padilla and so many more.

To my clients, thank you for your loyalty and confidence in my company, my product, and me. Without you, I would not be writing about my life story. Thank you.

To Team Lewin, for the thousands of clients who rely on us to make them look fantastic every year. I would not have been able to do this on my own. From scheduling appointments, to tailoring, to assisting in the day-to-day demanding schedules. and at times my direct ways to get things done. Thank you.

Today's work is the down payment for our future success.

To my beautiful wife, Jamie, for listening to all my dreams and ambitions and more dreams. For always doing what needs to get done to better us in life and in business. To always sharing your food, even when I know you really don't want to. To being the best cheerleader a man can ask for. For having faith and confidence in anything I do. Thank you for being my best friend, my lover, my confidant, and my wife. And, I am looking forward to our beautiful life together.

Make things happen for you, not to you.

ABOUT THE AUTHOR

Art Lewin is the owner and creative director of Executive Clothiers, one of the nation's premier bespoke clothiers.

Mr. Lewin is considered one of the leading experts on direct marketing, corporate image consulting, and the leading bespoke clothier to California's most prominent corporate stars and some of Hollywood's celebrities.

Mr. Lewin has been featured in the *Los Angeles Times*, CNN TV, the *Wall Street Journal, GQ, Beverly Hills Lifestyle Magazine, HispanicBusiness,* FOX 11 News, *Entrepreneur, Esquire, Los Angeles Business Journal, CSQ,* American Express, *Inc. Magazine,* ClubCorp, the *Hollywood Reporter, Confidential,* and numerous other publications, television, and radio.

ART LEWIN'S RÉSUMÉ

The Guru of Custom Clothing. **MyFoxLA**

America's Premier Custom Clothier. **American Express**

Winner Best Custom Tailors in Los Angeles. **Fox News 11**

Voted #1 Custom Clothier in Los Angeles. **L.A. Downtown News**

California's Businessman of the Year. **Wall Street Journal**

Top 50 fastest minority-owned businesses in LA. **Los Angeles Business Journal**

Nominated as Businessman of the Year. **California Chamber of Commerce**

Top 100 National Hispanic Entrepreneurs. **Hispanic**

One of the Best Dressed Men in America. **Esquire**

Listed on the national prestigious Inc. 500/5000 list. **Inc. Magazine**

Today, Art Lewin Bespoke is one of the leading custom clothiers in the country. We plan, coordinate, and maintain your wardrobe, so you are perfectly attired for any occasion. For more than two decades, we've catered to the area's corporate stars and to some of Hollywood's celebrities, and many other industry titans. As a second-generation clothier, Mr. Lewin says that our clients tell us that our workmanship, knowledge, attention to detail, and service make it readily apparent why we have been able to establish such a loyal following, with an impressive 94 percent client retention rate.

Mr. Lewin sits on the executive committee and chairs the membership committee at the City Club Los Angeles. He's also the founder of Professional Business Network (PBN), a group with more than 10,000 online members.

Mr. Lewin resides in Beverly Hills with his wife Jamie. In his spare time, he enjoys time with his kids, fine dining, socializing, working out, world travel, daily reading, daily learning, and many weekend getaways. If you would like to learn more about Art Lewin, please don't hesitate to ask art@artlewin.com.

FROM ORPHAN TO CEO

"I believe we were created for greatness, not mediocrity, that we are to live our lives accordingly, striving to be agents of change, as we attempt to leave this world a better place than we found it."

—Unknown

What is the most powerful language to create success? By language, I mean way of thought. My life's work will be a reflection of this quote by the unknown philosopher. For me, it is about being of influence and creating greatness in others. There's no purpose in life, if it is only to serve yourself.

The inner voice you argue with will deny this is true. It will tell you to create your own world of happiness. That you can do it on your own. But tell me, who is happy alone?

There are people you will need to come across in life to mold you into the story you will become. Everybody you meet can be of value to many others. Their life lessons of the right and wrong ways will help you to decide your life path. Their stories can inspire you to take action in your life.

For that to take place, you must first find out what that value is that you possess, your gift to the world, and your passion that you might never discover. I think too many people are distracted by the darkness of life to really see the potential within themselves. This, I hope, will be my change I bring to the world.

I didn't always believe this way, though. I was selfish; and in some ways, I still am. I walk into battle every day, as I step in front of that glass bathroom mirror, facing the eyes of my real, true self; still questions unanswered about who I am, about who I will become.

All my life I grew up not knowing my true identity. I would make up stories of my past to tell the new friends and acquaintances at the schools I'd attend.

Life, you could say, was anything but normal…

I was orphaned at 18 months when I was abandoned and left in a car with my 11-month-older sister. We were put into foster care, where I was adopted and returned by seven different families before finally being accepted into a family, with my sister, for the final time at almost four years old. Foster care was pretty much a blur to me, other than three engraved memories I can't seem to forget.

I couldn't have been more than three years old, and I'm watching my foster dad drink his beer from a glass, brown bottle, similar to those you see most beers come in these days. He's watching TV on his favorite, old, torn-up, brown recliner, feet up on an ottoman, remote controller on the left, beer on the right. He calls me over to play with him. I rush over, and as I reach his recliner, he hands me his glass bottle, smiles, and waits for me to grab it.

Not knowing the contents, as I'm just a toddler, I drink from the cold, brown bottle and immediately start choking on the foaming beer, as it burns my small throat. He sits there laughing in his recliner, almost falling over from the amazing story he'll be able to tell his wife when she gets home.

It's cold. It's dark. There's a window high above me. I can't reach it. The wind keeps blowing in more and more howling, winter air. I'm sleeping on the dusty, hardwood floor, shivering from the cold breeze that doesn't seem to ever have an end. My foster parents sold my bed earlier that day, for who knows what, so my bed that night was the empty floor. Sleeping didn't much exist that night, as I awoke early to an insect crawling into my left ear. I spent the remainder of the night paranoid that bugs were crawling all over me.

My final memory from living in foster care is actually a positive one. We were indoors—my sister, one other child, and me. The kitchen area was small, but it had a nook, which I remember had four, tall barstools placed in front. We were never allowed on them. But one day, all three of us kids got to sit on the barstools to eat our lunch—peanut butter and jelly sandwiches! I really liked the barstool I was on, because the seat would spin when I twisted.

It felt like an hour had passed before I finished my half sandwich, after all the spinning I did. It always brings a smile, thinking of that day.

Once adopted for the last time, things seemed to get better, at least for a while. I remember the first time I went to my new parents' house on Nectarine Ct. in Lake Elsinore, California. It was a two-story house that had what looked like a half-orange as a window, as we drove into the driveway.

Social workers would tell each potential adopting family that I would most likely have learning disabilities. The reason was because I didn't speak to anyone. The only person I would speak to was my older sister, Anna. I'd whisper in her ear, and she would be my voice. She was the only thing constant in my life. I had lost my mother, my father, everything, and everyone I knew, other than her. Whom could I trust at this point? Everyone who showed me a smile, or anything close to what you would call love, ended up leaving me or returning me, like an unwanted birthday toy.

I held my sister's hand, as I walked into my new parents' house. I immediately noticed the gray stairs in front of me. I had never seen stairs before, and they intrigued me. I didn't get much time that day to explore, as right away my sister and I were ushered into the living room. On the coffee table near the couch I was sitting on, I noticed a clear, glass bowl, full of candy! All kinds of different colors; my favorite was blue. I whispered to my sister to ask if I could have a piece. The adults were just a few feet away in the kitchen, talking grown-up stuff and looking at paperwork.

My sister approached my soon-to-be mother and father with my request and, of course, they obliged. I was so excited, rushed over, and grabbed two pieces, one in each little hand. I had a habit of getting one for me, and saving one for later. I believe they were M&M's, but I can't be too sure. I was only three and a half.

The social workers, I would also later find out, would tell the final adopted family about our habit of hiding food. According to them, the families we were with before our final adoption didn't think food was high on the priority list for us, and, as a result, my sister and I both suffered from malnutrition. My final family made sure that was never a problem moving forward.

The actual adoption process takes about a year to finalize, which was how I was able to be returned so many times. I would be adopted, drive my new parents crazy with my wild behavior, and they would end up returning me. Anytime between the adoptive parents taking a newly adopted child and the day they walk out of the courtroom with everything finalized, they can call the social worker and have the child picked up. Then off to another foster home the child goes.

I hope that process has changed by now, but that's what it was like for me.

Manny (third from left) and his sister on the day the adoption was finalized (1992). Picture provided courtesy of the author.

One family, I was later told, didn't like my acting out so much, so they used a lit cigarette on my chest as punishment for my bad behavior. I was only two. I still have a scar to this day. I didn't know what caused the scar, until I started asking questions about my adoption.

Being adopted, to me, is a blessing. Too many orphans fail to even get that chance. Some never get adopted at all. They go through their entire childhood jumping from foster home to foster home, wondering why they were never good enough to be loved. At 18, they're out on the street with not much more than a "good luck," with many ending up dead or in jail. The statistics are alarming. Look it up. They need mentors, guidance, support, and motivation. I hope to be part of that voice they need.

The next few years, after I was adopted, felt like heaven, at least to me, but not so much for my new parents. They had to figure out how to teach "foster care raised" children, who were not disciplined, how to be respectful members of society. To come from an environment where sometimes I was nothing more than a monthly paycheck, to being the light of someone's life, was a big change—a change I did not take well.

I acted out a lot; you could say I was a problem child. The scariest moment of my childhood would probably be when I was rushed to the emergency room, after my sister and I both put butter knives in a light socket in our house and electrocuted ourselves. The doctors checked us out and we were fine, with no serious injuries suffered.

School was just as bad, as I was always in trouble or in the principal's office, never listening to the teachers. The whole front office at any school I attended knew my mother by her first name. Yeah… it was *that* bad. Here are some of the things that happened.

Kicked out of preschool for dropping a TV on the teacher's toe.

Suspended from school multiple times.

Expelled from two different schools before even getting to high school.

Served detention, and Saturday school was almost a weekly routine.

Seated outside the fourth-grade classroom, literally! My desk was outside… of the classroom! It was called the "Manny Island."

I was also bullied in school, like most kids growing up. To me, it seemed like a normal part of life. It didn't faze me much, after learning that if I fought back, the bullies rarely wanted to continue using me as a punching bag.

I was always one of the small kids growing up; I graduated from high school at 135 pounds. I guess my small stature made me an easy target. My adopted father was similar. I don't really call him my adopted father. I usually just call him "Pops," so when I reference that name, I am referring to my adopted father.

You can really learn a lot about a person by understanding the people who raised them. Whether it's a mother, father, grandparent, aunt, uncle, brother, sister, friend, or mentor, your experiences in life will shape your character. You will either learn habits of success or danger zones you attempt to never cross. The key is to keep your mind open to the fact that you can learn both from anyone life puts alongside you on this journey.

Pops is one of those men. I've known him all my life as my father. I've seen him in no other light other than that. Even if my birth father were to show up at my doorstep today, Pops would still be my only father. He raised me since I was three and a half. He's shared his lessons of life as best he could teach them, from the lessons taught to him by his father and from what he has learned with the decades of life experience on this earth.

As I look back, as a dad today, I see Pops as a man who struggles daily to try and be the best father, husband, grandfather, and friend he is able to facilitate himself to be. I can't say that I would see Pops as a truly *happy* man. I see a lot of regret in his life. There are past mistakes that haunt him with the lost time he can never recover.

Sometimes you have to see the example put in front of you, as the path you cannot follow, one you must ignore to create your own. My purpose in life is not to just live, pay bills, and die. I want to create something that is more than I am, more than my story. I want people to be inspired to do great things in life, after hearing the path I forged to be where I am at today.

Luckily, I'm able to give you a story to read. At 16, I survived two near-death experiences. At 20, there was a third.

My first brush with death was simply because I was wearing the wrong color at a summer party. My friends and I showed up at a house party in Los Angeles wearing the opposite color of 99 percent of everyone else attending the party.

Long story short, we ditched the party quickly and walked to a nearby liquor store. We grabbed some snacks, walked back to our car to leave, and, as I was taking my seat in the back of the Honda Civic, another car was coming toward our direction. A reflection struck my eye from the passenger-side window. It was a silver gun, and the last thing I heard before ducking into the car at record speed was, "Where are those mother f***ers at?" The car drove by without seeing us (thank God for tinted windows), and we survived without a gunshot fired that night in our direction. Ten seconds later, and I could've been another inner-city, crime statistic for the eleven o'clock news.

The second near-death experience I had was a few months later, walking home one night around 1:00 AM. I'd always be out late with my friends on summer nights and would end up walking home by myself when everyone else was gone.

I was two miles from my house, when a car pulled up on my left. He was an older man in his late thirties, heavy set, close to 250–300 pounds. He asked if I needed a lift. He seemed nice and looked friendly, so I agreed to let him give me a ride, saving me 30 minutes of walking.

I got in his car, gave him general directions to where I lived, and we headed off. At the next light, a police cruiser was across from us. We were supposed to go straight, but he turned right. I asked him where he was going, as *my* house was the other way.

He put his hand on my left thigh and said, "Don't worry; it's ok. I'm taking a detour. Do you like that? Is that ok?" sliding his hand higher up my leg. I immediately pushed his hand away. He tried again, this time a little firmer. I pushed away again. He was starting to get angry.

I remembered what I had in my pocket, and it probably saved my life that night—my pocket knife! I always carried it on me that summer. I pulled it out, opened the blade, and put it to his face, telling him, "STOP THE CAR RIGHT NOW, AND LET ME OUT! I'M NOT PLAYING!"

He slammed on the brakes. I opened the door, and ran as fast as I could to the nearest neighborhood, hiding my shame of what I had just witnessed. My heart was racing. I felt sick. I had no clue what to do. Do I run home? Tell Pops what happened? Was this man following me?

I never looked back. I don't know which way he went. All I knew was I never saw his face again. I walked the rest of the way home that night. Later I stared at the ceiling in my room for hours. I never spoke of that night or the house party to Pops, so he'll be finding out when he reads this.

You might have noticed that I reference Pops more than my mom. I guess we can dabble in that subject while we're here. I wish I could say I have a good relationship with my adopted mother. Her name is Cathy.

It wasn't always bad. I'm hoping it will get better. I guess you could say the relationship started to deteriorate once I moved in with Pops in seventh grade. Before that, I had been living with my two sisters (one blood, one born after we were adopted) and my mother.

My dad offered to have me stay at his place, where I could have my own room. Living with my mom, I shared a bedroom. I would be able to learn how to be a man. I was also having problems at school, so having a fresh start was something I really needed, and I accepted his offer.

Cathy and Pops had split when I was 12. All I remember is that one morning my mother was crying on the couch, my dad was gone, and I was off to school an hour later. I was living in a bubble.

Oblivious to the problems of my family, I was lost in my own little world of video games, wrestling, and Pokémon.

I moved in with my dad, where I finally had my own room! It was awesome! Pops went all out. I was surprised on move-in day with new matching furniture, a desk, new bed, and my room was painted my favorite color blue! I was on cloud nine! We had a blast for about the next year, when, you could say, life got flipped upside down… again.

It was a sunny December day in Anaheim. I was at Dale Junior High School, eighth grade. I was called to the office. The principal is there with a police officer, who tells me, "Son, you're going to have to come with me."

I asked if I was in trouble. He assured me that I was not and that someone at the station would be able to tell me further what's going on. I got in the back of the police cruiser and the back seat, I found out, was plastic! There were arm cutouts in the seat, for an easy fit when someone has his or her hands cuffed behind their back. I decided to play along, as if I'm arrested, and I put my hands behind my back. Really, I was just trying to look cool to my friends, who were looking at me through the fence by the front office, as I was being taken away.

The officer noticed my immaturity and started to give me a lecture on how it's not cool to be in the back of his squad car. "Today, you're not in trouble, but you don't want to be in that seat with real handcuffs on, my friend."

What ended up happening was that Child Protective Services took me away from my family. I was placed in yet *another* foster home, Orangewood Foundation in Orange, California.

I was told absolutely nothing, as I was being dropped off in a white van, by myself. I had no clue where any of my family was at the time. Later, I was reunited with my two sisters. I felt like the one who had to take charge of things. My sisters were scared, so I was their comfort. I kept telling them everything would be fine. I didn't have a clue if anything actually was.

The place felt like jail. I had to sit in a waiting room for what felt like hours; then change all my clothes to the matching outfits of the facility, which were gray sweats and a gray sweater that didn't fit. I was placed in a room with guys who were in similar situations, I guess. I didn't talk to anyone to learn their stories, but I'd overhear a conversation or two. Some had been there for quite a while.

I didn't stay too long, though, as Uncle Andy, Cathy's brother, came to pick us up. I remember the green, gift-wrapped presents in the back of my uncle's SUV, which reminded me that this whole debacle occurred around Christmastime.

We ended up spending Christmas that year with my uncle, where I remember getting a super-cool silver and blue scooter with shocks in the back, so bouncing on it was fun. We were reunited with my mom about that time.

I wasn't given any answers about why this happened. I was left in the dark; all I knew was that I was not able to see my dad for months. Later, it became supervised visits; then, after what felt like years in the "system" again, we were free.

High school flew by quickly for me. I didn't make much of an impact, outside of getting straight A's for one semester and becoming student of the month my sophomore year. These achievements were, in reality, to prove my critics (my mother) wrong, even going as far as to make a contract that I had Cathy sign, saying she would give me $100 if I got straight A's. I did it, went to collect, and she said the contract was null and void, since I had moved in with my father after the contract was signed.

I really lost motivation for school at that point. I did all the hard work, the extra credit, completed homework on time, studied for tests, to hit my goal. But my accomplishments were belittled by the one person who should have had my back, my mother.

After that, I barely skated by in school; I almost didn't graduate my senior year, as I would always skip first period. Even Pops was skeptical of me getting my diploma, until graduation day. Hardly anyone believed in me at that time in my life, not even me. College, at that point, was not in my foreseeable future.

I did have one thing going for me at that time though—my girlfriend, Nancy. We had just started dating the month I graduated. She was a junior. I was a senior. I met her through a mutual friend, and little did I know the effect this woman would have on my life.

I decided to join the Navy after high school, but my presence was short-lived. After graduating from boot camp in Illinois, Pops brought my cell phone to my graduation to have for the weekend to call my girlfriend, as we could only communicate via snail mail back then. I was supposed to be flying out to my training school for my job in the Navy within three days of graduating, so I thought I could easily hide my phone until I shipped out. There was a ban on having phones on the base by the captain, so having one was a big no-no!

My training got delayed a couple of weeks, and I ended up getting caught with my phone, not too long after my delay. I was arrested by the military police, told to write a statement on the situation, and later put on suicide watch for my lack of communication, after being humiliated in front of my peers, for a simple cell phone.

I'm not the type of person to filter my thoughts, so I wrote a long, detailed letter to the captain, venting my emotions on the wasted focus of this ridiculous ban. I came face to face with the captain of the base during a captain's mast, which is like court for the military. The captain read my letter to everyone in the room, which included every available chief officer and petty officer on the base, dozens in attendance. After reading it, he proceeded to give me an order of 45 days' restriction, 45 days extra duty, half-pay times two, and then says, "GET THE F*** OUT OF MY NAVY!"

So, I'm back to square one—home, unemployed, but all is not lost. I still have my supportive girlfriend who stuck by my side through every step of the chaotic past six months.

Before I went to the Navy, I sat down with Pops and told him I was going to marry this girl. We had only been dating for fewer than two months at the time, but I knew something was different with her. She wasn't like the others. My dad laughed at me, thinking I was just talking crazy from the lust of a new relationship.

Maybe I wasn't so crazy. That girlfriend of two months is now my wife of more than 12 years, and we have three beautiful children to call our own. My first son, Isaac, was born less than a year after

I came back from the Navy. I came home in December; Isaac was born the next November.

You could say I grew up pretty fast. I married my high school sweetheart, was on my own by 18, and became a father by 19. I was an entrepreneur by 21, father of two by 22, started my second business at 24, named "One of the Best" by Facebook at 25, and in the five years since, my work has been featured on NBC, Bloomberg Radio, *Huffington Post,* and I'm a paid consultant to close to a thousand brands worldwide!

All this might never have been, if I hadn't survived my third near-death experience, age 20, shortly after Isaac was born.

We were heading to Laughlin, Nevada, for a family summer vacation with my one-year-old son. That morning, my abdomen felt like it was on fire. I started to sweat, and within hours I was throwing up every 30 minutes. I headed to the emergency room and within minutes of arrival, I was on a stretcher headed into emergency surgery.

I had appendicitis and my appendix needed to be removed. It could burst at any moment, and I could die. I had surgery, woke up the next day with family around me, and spend the next couple of days in the hospital recovering.

If I had been halfway to Laughlin and my appendix had burst, there's a high probability I would not be here today, telling you my story. Maybe the universe does have plans for me after all. I know a few people who sure did.

One, in particular, was a man by the name of Gale Oliver. He was my supervisor at the company I had started working at in

2007. He discovered me, invested his time and resources, and shared his stories of struggle with me; I could relate to him. We had similar life experiences, and, I didn't know it at the time, I had my first mentor.

This was the key that unlocked my potential. Mentorship! He was someone to bounce ideas off, someone who had been in the trenches where I was. He was where I wanted to be, and he wanted to see me succeed. A mentor gives guidance, counsel, points you in the right direction, and keeps you challenged, so you don't fall into the pit of mediocrity. Gale was that man for me. We started off mornings with motivation and a prayer.

He is where I get the catch-phrase, "Too Blessed to Be Stressed!"

Each morning I'd come into work, walk by his desk, and ask how he's doing. Like clockwork, his response would always be, "Too Blessed to Be Stressed!"

He instilled in me the concept of looking at life as always full. Full of blessings to point to for motivation and inspiration. My family was that drive for me. My underlying desire was to be something great, for them. I wanted to stop building someone else's dream and start to build my own.

He knew I was destined for more. While I only saw how far I could go in the company I was at, Gale was already seeing me running companies of my own. Soon, situations became clear for me to branch out on my own, which I did in 2009, walking away from a comfortable income to pursue my own dream.

I must have had a delusional amount of confidence, as I made this decision while my wife was six months pregnant with our second child, Xavier. I made the leap, jumped into entrepreneurship blindfolded with both feet tied together, and soon enough… I crashed and burned.

Within a year, I went from having a luxury apartment, a $50,000 Lexus, taking my family on vacations every other month, to losing it all. I was homeless, with a family of four to support. With nowhere to go, I turned to family, to my mom, Cathy.

We overstayed our welcome, and, after just a few months, we ended up on the street again, this time by the grandmother to my children, and the person I called Mom. There was no explanation, no reason, just a knock on the door on a Saturday morning by my uncle, informing me to vacate the premises within a week. I tried to ask for an explanation from Cathy, but she refused to give one.

That day resulted in me not talking to her for more than five years. I've since buried the hatchet and we began to talk again. I invited her to Mother's Day brunch one morning, as we both sat at church, the only place our paths ever seemed to cross anymore.

Throughout the adversities I've faced in life, I've discovered a few simple concepts that have given me the will to always keep going, no matter the situation in front of me.

Living my life #TooBlessedToBeStressed.

Having people in my circle of influence who are smarter than I am.

Marrying my opposite in life to balance my ego and weaknesses.

Listening to my gut feeling when opportunities present themselves.

Being a sponge for knowledge.

Mentorship.

If you live by these simple truths in life, the hustle code will automatically embed in your DNA, as a result of your actions!

I started my branding agency, shortly after being kicked out on the street by my mother. I ended up living in the backyard of someone's house with my wife and two sons, both under five. They had converted an area to a one-bedroom living space, which included a small kitchen and bathroom. I couldn't complain, as anything was better than having my family live on the streets.

I stayed there for about a year, kept things as low budget as I could, while I built my company. I noticed after making all that money years before, I had nothing to show for it once everything crashed around me. I didn't save; I spent like it always would be there, but now I play by different rules. I had to raise a family of four on one income for quite a while, until we added my baby girl, Ava Navelle, to our family in 2014, which then made it five!

Being a father and entrepreneur can be difficult. Life as a CEO is tough, definitely not for the weak minded. The freedom it gives you, though, can't be matched. I get to enjoy my kids' sports whenever they play. I get to go on field trips without worry of having to ask for time off.

There are a lot of ups and downs in this lifestyle, especially when it comes to a stable income. There were many times in the first five years of growing my branding agency that I had no clue where I'd find a way to put food on the table. Business slows, funds dry up, and I had to choose between food and electricity. It always seemed to work out, though. Trusting a higher power to provide, when faith is limited, has been crucial for my confidence to be successful.

Whatever that motivation to you might be, focus on it. Embrace it. Use it to power you through the downs you'll face in life. We all get them; misery is no stranger. Everyone has a gift, a purpose, and a value that only he or she can bring to the world.

What is that value you possess? What will you pass on to the next generation, as a way to bring a better understanding to this phenomenon that we call life? I strongly urge you find a mentor. Find the gift you were given, nurture it, care for it, grow it, and expose it to the experience of challenge. This will be your purpose in life. If you develop a valuable skill from this passion, it can become your business.

Another thing you must understand to be successful is that you and your business will only go so far on your own. You cannot do this alone. You will need someone to help you fight the voice in your head that will try to keep you from becoming the person you were born to be. Every great leader has a mentor; most have more than one. Find someone who is where you want to be; learn from him or her, become a sponge of knowledge to the world around you, and the resources they connect you with.

The next thing you need is a way to bring your value to the world. You will need to brand it and automate the process of finding people interested in what you have to offer. You can only be so many places at once, so the key to doing this right is to package it in a way that anyone worldwide can access it, even while you sleep! That is what I teach in my business: how to duplicate yourself with systems of automation.

The next tip is to start teaching. Start a blog, YouTube channel, Facebook group, mobile app, write a book, or something where you can organize and bring attention to your intellectual property. Put together a list of questions that clients ask or should ask when doing business with you and answer them in short videos, audios, or text. This will be your valuable content to give away for free.

While putting all this together, you will need to define your target market, who you want to reach with your message of value. If you have a business and are not sure how to go about this process or if you would like some help, for taking the time to read my story, I'd like to offer you my time. You can set up a free one on one with me at www.ChatWithManny.com, where I'll give you actionable tips about how to generate leads in your business using my unique strategies.

You can also download my free mobile app called "Learn With Manny" to stay up to date with all my latest strategies on lead generation and automation marketing. Just search for "Manny Lopez" in your favorite app store to find it quickly!

Thank you for taking the time to learn my story. Now that you know mine, I'd love to learn yours. I hope we can connect, as you never know who will be that next person you come across who will change your life.

I look forward to being a resource to you. Always remember: you are too blessed to be stressed!

"Life is measured in the people you share it with. Find that purpose in life, that drive that defines you."
— Manny Lopez

Manny helps create & enhance experts with unique lead generation & automation marketing strategies. A husband and father of 3, he devotes his time to creating a lifestyle of being #TooBlessedToBeStressed while managing his network of over 20,000 business professionals worldwide!

Within his business specialty, he 1st understands your business model, target market, and challenges you're facing. Once discovered, he'll develop a unique way to automate your sales process and message of value to reach the specific market that works best for YOU. Here are some of those ways:

- Universal Mobile Apps

- Mobile App Marketing

- Featuring your business on ABC, NBC, CBS, & FOX

- Featuring your business on his TV show

- Featuring your business on his radio show

+ much more!

Currently, he is a paid consultant on lead generation to over 1000 brands worldwide including: celebrities, entertainers, entrepreneurs, best-selling authors, speakers, coaches, network marketing companies, affiliates, attorneys, doctors, and hundreds of small business professionals from around the world!

He's worked with influencers such as:

- Les Brown (#1 Motivational Speaker)

- Greg S. Reid (Film-maker & Best-Selling Author)

- Frank Shankwitz (Make-A-Wish Foundation)

- Bill Walsh (America's Business Expert)

- Tai Lopez (Serial Entrepreneur, Social Influencer)

+ Hundreds of professionals worldwide!

His work has been featured on NBC, The Huffington Post, Bloomberg Radio, a CEO Space International graduate, INC Magazine and at 25, was named "One of the Best" by Facebook when they hit 1 million advertisers!

Connect with Manny at www.FromOrphanToCEO.com

PUNCH CARDS

LESSONS FROM BOXING, POKER, AND HARD WORK

ABEL ANDRADE

I recall standing along the edge of the gym at the Martin Luther King Recreation Center surrounded by the smell of sweat and old leather, holding a feeling of disappointment in my stomach. It appeared that, once again, I would not get a match today. The noise of the other contenders crashing against each other in the ring filled the tight space with palpable electricity. It had taken me months of training to get here, and I wanted to have my first amateur bout today and feel that same energy inside the ring myself. I would not wait another month.

I had traveled to Lynwood, California, from my hometown of Lawndale, because I was desperately seeking someplace where I could have my first boxing match. At about 15 years of age, I had recently received an athletic scholarship to Bishop Montgomery High School in Torrance, but the school didn't have a boxing program, so I had been traveling to this new gym for the past two weeks to train.

My father, Antonio Andrade, had been encouraging me for the many months of training leading up to this moment. He had been bolstering my spirits during the drive and keeping my hopes up that I would find a match today. He and I bonded while watching and talking about boxing. My father is a fearless man who came to the United States from Mexico and relentlessly worked to improve his family's situation. He always emphasized the value of hard work to me, and he felt I would learn that virtue through my boxing training.

Now, I was simply waiting to be paired with another boxer for a match. I walked over to the bout scheduling table and found my manager, who had been busy trying to negotiate to get me an opponent.

"Sorry, Abel. No one is agreeing to a match. The people I thought would agree said they didn't want to fight with someone they had already been training with the past couple of weeks," he said, exasperated. He silently noted the look of disapproval on my face by rubbing his forehead.

I looked around and saw the faces of those I had been sparring and training with the past few weeks. My local gym in Lennox didn't have a boxing ring, and many fighters traveled around looking for sparring partners... which led me to the gym in Lynwood.

As I looked around, I noticed an older-looking, African American boxer who hadn't been in the ring yet. He was maybe a few years older than me. He would be the one I would face. My manager tried to talk me out of it, warning me that he was an older boxer from a nearby gym. I was unsure of the outcome, but I was certain of my desire. I told him to set up the match. He sighed, gave me that exasperated look that says, "You can't be serious!" He saw the response in my unblinking eyes and reluctantly walked over to the bout table to set up the match.

Soon, I found myself stepping into the ring opposite this unfamiliar contender. A wave of exhilaration and uncertainty washed over me, but I reminded myself of my training and calmed my thoughts. The referee did the usual glove inspection, sportsmanship talk, and explained these amateur matches were being kept to three rounds. He quickly signaled for round one to begin.

I opened with an aggressive advance toward his corner and let a series of impulsive swings fly. I was testing my opponent, and he was dodging each attempt from a conservative stance, as he felt me out. My aggressive style was leaving me open, and he used those opportunities to rack up some quick points as he kept tagging me. By the end of the first round, we had each landed a few superficial punches and were both eager for the next round. I excitedly went back to my corner with an elevated heart rate. I was finally competing in my first amateur boxing match. I felt like nothing would defeat me.

Round two began in earnest, as each of us felt we now knew our opponent enough to launch our best offensive attack. After we circled each other for a few moments, I barreled forward again with a round of jabs, as he deftly glided backwards on his buoyant footwork. He ducked left and came up again with a left hook to my side, which sent me off balance for a second, but I was otherwise unfazed. The next moment he was on the offensive, and I raised my gloves to guard from his powerful punches.

It seemed to last unbearably long. I couldn't keep my vision on him due to this flurry of punches, some of which were meeting my face through my gloves. As my guard wavered, I felt a terrible blow to my face that sent me reeling. It shook my whole body and my legs almost gave, as I staggered to the edge of the ring for something to lean on. Luckily, the second round ended before he could follow up on that onslaught. I looked over and saw that he held a 12-point lead. Maybe a win wasn't in the cards for me today.

I regrouped in my corner before the final round, hearing words of encouragement from my father. I knew my aggressive approach wasn't going to overpower this man; he was bigger than me. I would have to be smarter and work harder than him. When the bell rang for the start of round three, I set my strategy in motion.

I watched him carefully as he stepped forward, setting up another round of his powerful jabs. I stepped back, ducked, and countered, landing a punch underneath his impressive reach. I knew it would be a grind, but if I could concentrate and keep up this slower, deliberate strategy, I could earn enough points for a win. Luckily, my opponent made the mistake of underestimating me, due to the hits he landed in the second round. He wasn't ready for me to adapt this quickly.

This new methodical strategy gave me the opportunity to avoid his blows and land several counterpunches in a row, reversing the pace of the match. I kept my focus and single-minded determination on my defense and countering his attacks. I noticed he was starting to show signs of tiring. His next jab revealed an opening, and I took it. I connected a solid right cross to his chin and knocked him down. An utter look of surprise painted his face, as he quickly stumbled back to his feet. I thought, *I can win this, if I land one more of those!* I positioned myself to counter his next punch, but just then the final bell rung.

We breathlessly shook hands, and the sting of disappointment surged as the referee announced him as the winner. As I walked back to my corner to recover, my manager and father offered sincere words of encouragement.

The opponent's manager was walking by and stopped when he saw me. He gave me a pat on the back, "You've got balls, kid, you know that?"

"Uh, thanks… but I lost," I muttered.

My manager said, "Why are you so disappointed? Did you even look at the final score? That was a narrow match. A valiant performance!"

I glanced over and saw 15–14 on the board. In that final round, I had returned from a deep point deficit to lose by only one point.

The opponent's manager added, "I couldn't believe it when you entered the ring at first, because my guy is 27 years old, and you're, what… in high school? But you worked hard and showed us what you're made of in there."

Life follows a similar trajectory to that match. The win is in the hard work and not the points. It's in how you grow after taking a hit, not if you get knocked down. If life is a boxing match, then it will inevitably land some devastating blows to all of us. Even if you think you can hide in your corner of the ring, life will find a way to catch you off guard and put obstacles in your way. You have to choose to put yourself in the thick of it and fight, even when the odds are against you. You'll want to lash out, but there is no winning in being reckless and impulsive. Working hard with a methodical, deliberate approach is how you *earn* the win.

Getting knocked down happens to everyone. Just get up, dust yourself off, and decide that the final bell hasn't rung, yet. In a boxing match, there are a limited number of rounds, but in life you decide when they end. Prepare yourself for the struggle that life can bring with training, hard work, learning from mentors in your life, and keeping your eye on the long-term prize.

GRATITUDE

I grew up in a rough neighborhood. I had friends who joined gangs, got into crime, and some even died from gunshot wounds. I could have easily been swept into that culture, if it were not for my wonderful parents who helped me avoid the local public high schools. You've already met my father, the solid foundation of my family and a role model for me. He taught me that I can only achieve better things when I push myself to go further than I think I can. Early on, though, he was the one pushing me, because I had not yet learned how to push myself. He taught me to be resolute and proud of my roots.

My mother is a giver and a caretaker, always thinking of others before herself. She is still very talkative and loves having visitors, especially on Sunday. She inspires love and passion in those around her. Both of my parents are hard workers, which was a virtue instilled deeply within me. So, despite lapses later on, I was able to draw on that instinct to pull me back from some of my deepest setbacks.

During my senior year in high school, a car accident left me with a separated shoulder and a fractured humerus bone. I was unable to compete. I had already committed to Occidental College in Los Angeles to play football… but, after the accident, my full-ride, sports scholarship was reduced. As I graduated from high school in 1993, my dreams of going to college disintegrated before my eyes, because I would no longer have the financial support afforded me by my athletic ability.

After a year of recovery, I settled on joining the Marine Corps Reserves. I served for six years, until the year 2000. During this period, I continued my boxing training and found a new hobby in poker, which absolutely captivated me. I continued to compete in amateur boxing fights and kept up my training with plans to go professional by the age of 22. However, I later accidentally dropped that goal, because I kept being drawn away by this fascinating game of cards.

I enthusiastically dove into poker and learned all I could about it. I found myself to be a natural at the psychological aspect of the game. I could read on their faces when people were bluffing, and I could read their motivations in the chips and choices, as if it were written in plain English. I read books and magazines about poker strategy and even learned enough about statistics and probability to be dangerous at the table. I often played small-stakes games, at first, $100 to $200 buy-ins.

Something about the atmosphere of late-night poker games invites the use of alcohol. I certainly drank my fair share of it and began to develop a habit of late-night partying. With my success at the card table, I began to believe there was an easier way to earn that proverbial win. Poker looked like a shortcut from where I sat back then. It was certainly easier than boxing.

About the time I forgot my professional boxing goals, I started working at Aurora Electronics in Marina del Rey to earn extra money over my Marine Corps stipend. It was a computer parts distributor, and I worked there as a production controller. It was an hourly job that had me punching my time card every day. The days were slow and repetitive. There was no excitement in this daily grind, like there was in my frequent poker games. However, there was a beautiful woman in sales, named Amy, who caught my eye. That was enough to keep me there. We hit it off and were married a few years later.

Amy was about five years older than me and from a very different socioeconomic background. Her family was not a fan of my boxing training, especially her father who was a doctor and had seen the head trauma of some former boxers. But Amy saw something in me, and she even became a kind of mentor; she was a source of inspiration for me to push myself to grow as an individual. We had two beautiful twin boys, Robert and Jacob, who are the joys of my life.

Not long after I married her, I took my gambling habit to another level… or should I say that it took me to another level? It is hard to recall if I was in control or if the cards were. I began consistently spending late nights in casinos and risking hundreds of dollars on a single hand. And when I wasn't playing, I was watching professionals play the game on television. I was building a respectable bankroll from all my success in poker, and I kept having the urge to increase the stakes.

At first, Amy was silent about me returning occasionally in the middle of the night. My pride from my Mexican culture also made it difficult for me to open up with her and honestly communicate what I was doing. I think I knew I was falling into the temptation of easy money, and that contradicted what my father had always taught me about hard work. I believe that internal friction caused me to suppress admitting my true activities to Amy and to others.

In 2008, the growing stress from my gambling habits, my immature and selfish behavior, and the impact of the economic crisis on Amy's job, all culminated in a series of arguments that saw us grow distant. We separated informally in 2008 for a few months, then tried to reconcile. We tried several marriage counselors, but I let my selfishness prevent me from communicating and showing my gratitude to this woman who had actually taught me so much. Ultimately, we filed for divorce in 2009.

In retrospect, I carry the fault in this failure, and it was because I forgot a simple lesson from my mother of showing gratitude to influential loved ones in your life. Amy gave 110 percent to our relationship, and I was not giving it everything I had. I was letting the temptation of poker pull me away from the truly valuable things. She was good to me and helped me grow as a person, and I did not reciprocate in the ways that I could have. I had forgotten how to show I was grateful to her for that.

This was the first blow in life's boxing match that really knocked me down and made me feel like a failure. I slipped into a dark age of my life; I became depressed. I had it all: a big house, beautiful family, and stability. It should have been everything anyone could reasonably ask for, especially considering the lower socioeconomic background I came from.

You have to be grateful to your friends and family for the support they provide, because there is no substitute for that. I think back to this round of my life whenever I am struggling, and now I am sure to remember to remind my loved ones of how grateful I am to them.

DELAYED GRATIFICATION

The casino atmosphere provided a thrill and a refuge all at once; there was no stress from work or relationships to distract me there. I could forget about all that and just let myself get lost in the cards. After a few months, I had become a regular. I would always go in and head straight to the poker table; I didn't engage in any other form of gambling, because poker was unique.

If you place a bet with a bookie on some sporting event, you truly have no influence on the outcome. Poker wasn't quite gambling to me, because there was legitimate skill involved that separated the players. How the cards come up is chance. But you don't play the cards, you play the other people, and that gives the best players some control over the outcome.

Reading people is a skill, and I learned to see how the other players spoke with body language, tells, nervousness, and confidence. I could see right through bluffs. The signals were everywhere, from on their faces, to their past actions, to how many chips they held at the moment of a surprising call. Skillfully interpreting these signs reduced the influence of chance involved in the dealing of cards. When and how I folded, called, and raised was entirely in my power. And if I could read the other players, then I had a definitive edge.

I noticed a couple of guys who were at the poker table as consistently as I was. They were good players too; I think we exchanged winning and losing hands fairly evenly among one another. It was much harder to get a read from their expressions. One late night after a round of poker, I went to get a drink. The two of them were already at the bar and waved me over and ordered me a drink. Their names were Mike and John. Two fellow poker enthusiasts, like me, who enjoyed the skill of the game. We became fast friends and saw a lot of one another during the next few months at the casino.

Meeting Mike and John marks the point when my casino habit started snowballing and when my relationship with Amy really started to strain. I was frequently going on late-night and occasional all-night gambling escapes. Walking in the front door at 3:00, or even 6:30, in the morning would naturally concern anyone. I was still working full-time and enrolled at a community college, working toward a second degree. My gambling habit was growing to the point where I would sometimes skip my college classes, which eventually led to putting that degree on hold. I never skipped work because of my gambling, though.

One night Mike and John started asking me if I did any other sort of gambling. They said they had a golden opportunity, a "slam dunk bet," as they put it. They knew someone on the inside of a sports game who was guaranteeing a certain outcome. I told them that I didn't bet on games, but they reassured me this was in the bag already. They had assurance from the insider that it was a no-risk proposition. Despite my doubts, I took the leap and placed my bet with Mike and John, thinking I would simply need to wait a short while before I received a large payout. Of course, it never happens like that.

A week later, I arrived at the casino to play a round of poker when Mike and John rushed toward me in complete panic. They said the sports bet had flopped. I was shattered. This wiped out the substantial bankroll I had built during the past couple of years. I felt everything spiraling out of control in my head, as if taking a solid right hook to the temple that knocked me to my knees.

In desperation, I took out loans from a bookie to try to win my money back at the high-stakes poker table. But in my state of emotional recklessness, I only ended up losing that money too. I sank into a depression for months. I owed about $12,000 to underground lenders, and the only way I knew how to earn it back was with poker, but gambling was what got me into this mess. The allure of fast money and easy success shimmered like an oasis in the desert. Even though I knew the oasis wasn't truly there, I had reached out toward it and willingly drank sand.

After a few weeks of calming myself and collecting my thoughts, I was back at the casino, only to earn back some money for a down payment on this loan. I was sticking to the low-stakes tables, where I had reliably built my hefty bank account before. I couldn't afford any more risk than that. I was bringing in a bit of money and making weekly payments to that bookie, but as the weeks passed, and the cards dried up, I missed some payments.

I left the casino after another night of modest poker winnings. I crouched into my car, shut the door, and looked down to get my key.

Tap. Tap. Tap.

I looked up, startled by the imminent sound. There were two men, on my right and my left, outside my car windows staring at me through their dark sunglasses. The one at my window tapped again. I rolled down the window.

He said, "We were in the neighborhood. You have the payment?"

"Not yet, I'm working on it," I muttered.

"And yet you are here gambling?" he asked incredulously.

"That's how I'm getting the money. You'll get it, soon."

"The boss needs $5,000 now," he insisted.

"I don't have that much money right now." I looked at the man on my right, who let out a loud huff and looked upset at my admission. I felt a strong, cold grip on my shoulder.

The first man said, "We need that money by the end of the week. You got that?"

I can read people. What I saw in his gesture was not a bluff, and it terrified me to my core.

I doubled my efforts at the low-stakes, low-risk tables and buckled myself in for a grind. At these tables I could reliably win, but it would be slow going. After a few more months, I paid off the loan. That encounter leveled my head in a jarring way. It was like a solid right hook to the head that made my ears ring and my sight blur, until I'd lost all sense of what direction I was facing. When that was settled, I vowed never to fall for the allure of easy shortcuts again.

From then on, I would delay gratification and set my goals for the long-term payout.

I would earn my personal wins with hard work: punching time cards from here on out. Slinging poker cards appeared like an easy shortcut, but I paid a higher cost later on. That round of my life might have temporarily bested me, but there were plenty more rounds to go. Just like after the difficult round in my first amateur boxing match, I regrouped, adapted my strategy, and put my deliberate, methodical plan of punching time cards to work.

HARD WORK

It was time to look straight ahead and never look back. I swore off gambling, though the temptation never fully goes away. I decided to make something more of myself—a career that I could be proud of and that my kids could be proud of too. So, I hit the pavement looking for honest work, and I tapped my old network of friends to ask around. Though difficult, I dusted myself off, took things one day at a time, and I soon found plenty of opportunities.

I had already obtained my bachelor's degree through hard work and sheer determination in 2004. I had worked in the information technology (IT) field for many years during my poker days, but the passion for that career had left me. Now, I was working two or three jobs at once to get back on my feet and get a bit of a safety fund into my bank account.

I was working at a call center during the day and as a waiter at night, when I reached out to my high school friend, Angelo. He had been doing well for himself at a large corporation and said he knew of an opportunity with his boss, Pablo. They had met while working at a marketing agency. Pablo was now the vice president of sales and marketing at a Fortune 500 company, and Angelo was able to introduce me us and set up an interview. It turns out the company was hiring for entry level Hispanic brand ambassadors through a hiring agency.

I interviewed and was called back immediately with an offer. I would be doing community outreach and brand promotion among certain demographics in the Los Angeles area. It meant speaking with people on a daily basis, both store owners and retailers, in addition to customers. I was always good at interacting with people, but the sales aspect of this position was a new skill I would have to learn. The practice I had in reading people from my pokers days was of great use during negotiations, in the stores, on the streets, and in the corporate meeting rooms.

My new attitude and determination toward hard work must have been noticed, because I was promoted to the senior Hispanic brand ambassador role in eight months. I was supervising a team of about eight people, and we were expanding the reach of this marketing push to help our products have a greater impact in the Hispanic community. The effort began to bear fruit, and the company decided, four months later, that it wanted to bring the program under its own control, rather than managing it via a hiring agency. The company liked the results, but, in order to control costs, the leaders decided to keep only the best three ambassadors out of the thirty-five they had hired through the agency.

I was one of the three who made the cut and was hired full-time. I got a new title: Hispanic execution manager. It was obviously new, because they didn't have time to think of a name for the position that did not bring the image of an ax and a black hood to mind.

No one ever claimed Human Resources was good at marketing. Anyway, I was ecstatic. The reward from delayed gratification had finally come, and it was sweeter than any poker pot I had ever won!

I focused on my new role assisting the sales team in gaining an understanding of the Hispanic market. I became a prominent influencer among retailers and customers in our region. Pablo mentioned that a new opportunity had opened up in Denver to be the Desert Mountain region manager. He said he thought I had what it took for the position and encouraged me to apply. I thought he was just being complimentary, because I still felt inexperienced. I applied, mostly just to humor him and to show some initiative, but I never really believed that I would have a chance at the role. But, just like in boxing, I had to put myself in the ring first, if I wanted to be a contender. Sometimes you'll be surprised at certain capabilities, which you didn't even realize you had.

I went to Denver at the end of 2014 and am now going on my third year as the Desert Mountain region manager. I have made a great career with a respectable salary at a Fortune 500 company. I'm proud of how I landed on my feet, after life knocked me down. Restarting from a simple determination to take the next chapter of my life one day at a time, I made the choice to put in the hard work of punching those time cards and making it closer to my goal, one step at a time.

The hardest part of that decision was forfeiting my four or five opportunities per week to see my kids, who were still in LA. I call them every day and fly back for several weekends and holidays during the year to spend time with them. My next goal is to be able to move back to be a positive role model with a proud career and, more important, to be a father for them. Being apart from them these several years in Denver has been harder than any of my previous setbacks in poker, in relationships, and in boxing. But when I return to them, I want to bring the experienced character of a man who has endured setbacks and fought to overcome them.

This time in Denver has been a sorely needed time of soul searching for me. I have been able to reflect on the setbacks earlier in my life, and it has led to a lot a maturing in me. I am training again in the local gym for my next boxing match. I receive a fair amount of criticism for doing that now at the age of 41, but I am a fighter by nature. That part of me can't be rewritten, nor should it be. That is the part of me that saw me through some of my darkest times.

I have set a goal for myself of competing in a professional match by the end of the year. It is really less of a new goal and more of a goal I have rediscovered, after having forgotten about it during a long journey. It is a fitting closure to the tortuous series of struggles that brought me to the success and stability that I can now happily boast.

The story of my life has been a brawl from the beginning with my amateur boxing experiences, car accident setback, early university and sports career disappointments, to overcoming personal and relationship hurdles. Concluding this chapter of my life with a final professional boxing match is the best way to create meaning from all that.

§§§

From the struggles of difficult tribulations emerges a rich set of experiences to draw from to teach my children the valuable lesson that those events taught me. I will make sure to teach them to show gratitude to loved ones, to strive to delay gratification by working hard in the present moment in pursuit of a worthy goal, and to avoid the allure of temptations that only hold false promises.

I have learned to be more appreciative of my relationships with my family, with mentors such as Amy, and with dependable friends. Take the time to remind those around you of your gratitude toward them. Overcome the inhibition to communicate; instead, share your thoughts honestly with those people. Gratitude and communication are essential for healthy relationships. Give 100 percent of yourself to your relationships to put yourself in a position of success.

Don't let quick and easy temptations steer your actions, as I did with my gambling habit. It can easily spiral out of control. You are always at risk of losing more than you can possibly gain from those activities. Even if you gain some easy money, you risk losing your close relationships. No one is immune from those activities veering into dangerous territory. Take control of your own behavior, and practice the habit of delaying gratification. The rewards from being patient are sweeter and longer lasting.

I learned early on from my father that I had to work hard to succeed, and my boxing training was what solidified that lesson in me. As I drifted away from the regimented discipline of boxing toward poker, I forgot this lesson. I've since remembered its value, and I want to be sure that other people, including my kids, don't have to suffer the consequences of forgetting it, like I did.

The prize for the best contender is worth little, compared to the growth that comes from the effort of training and striving to achieve. Hard work pays off, because it's how you grow your resolve, sculpt your body, and mature your character into a stronger version of itself. That personal improvement stays with you longer than any trophy can.

Thank you, dear readers, for listening to what I've learned during my life of boxing, poker, and hard work. I believe there is a message of hope and courage that everyone can learn from. You are all capable individuals who can achieve great things, beyond what you currently imagine. You will be surprised by how talented you are, when you step out of your comfort zone and into the proverbial ring. Always strive for a worthy goal, whatever that might be for you, and I think you will enjoy an equally rewarding journey, as I have. If you remember the lessons of gratitude, communication, delayed gratification, and hard work, then your journey might be somewhat less rocky than mine.

Abel Andrade is the proud father of identical twin boys and an aspiring professional boxer. He has gained valuable experience in Hispanic Marketing, brand development and community outreach working for Fortune 500 company, Dr Pepper Snapple Group. His professional accolades have been featured in CASA magazine. As a member of the United Stars Marine Corps he was meritoriously promoted in boot camp and in his Military Occupational School for being number one in his class. He loves contributing to his community and helping others develop and grow professionally and in their personal lives. Born and raised in Los Angeles, he currently lives in Denver Colorado.

HEART OF AN UNDERDOG

EDDIE BORDENS

Many of you know me as the first-place winner from Grant Cardone's *Whatever It Takes* reality TV show, season 1. However, my hustle wasn't triggered by that achievement in itself, it was triggered back in 1988. That's when my hustle began.

I was living the American dream. I was about nine years old. I had a mother, father, brothers, and sister. We lived in a beautiful home in the city with the largest pool any kid could possibly want. I even had a dog named Spikey.

One day my father said goodbye and left for work. I never saw him again. Overnight, I became a statistic, "another Hispanic kid without his father." I still carry a lot of pain, questions, and rage! After the tragic loss of my father, our life crumbled; we lost it all. My father lost his life to cirrhosis of the liver. For a man who wasn't a heavy drinker, it was a bit of a surprise to all of us. But I guess it's not unheard of, especially to me and my family. It seemed to have hit us like a ton of bricks.

I was forced to move to Guadalajara, Mexico. My mother (my hero) had never worked outside the home in her life. At that time, my mother made the choice to move my older brother (by one year) and me to Mexico, where she had most of her family. It was a place she called home and she must have felt more comfortable raising my brother and me there. She adapted to her surroundings.

My mother is a perfect example of the saying, "Never give up." I've never understood how she did it, how she supported my brother and me all those years and gave us everything we ever needed and wanted. I have to say I lived a good life. I never had a need for something she couldn't or wouldn't buy for me—she is my hero.

I also adapted to my surroundings and quickly learned the "Mexican life." A few years passed, and I would go to school all morning and then run to work afterwards until about 8:00 p.m., plus I worked all day Saturday and Sunday. I landed my first full-time job making gold jewelry at the age of 14. Needless to say, a few months later, I was wearing more gold jewelry than an Italian version of Mr. T, but I was only 14–15 years old.

I quickly realized that to survive, I must adapt to my surroundings. Not having a father growing up forced me to master some skills—the skills of survival and hustle. And during the next 20 years, I learned to do it well. I am Edward Bordens, entrepreneur of life, and I'm on the path of discovering my full potential.

> "He uses statistics as a drunken man uses lamp posts—for support rather than for illumination."
> —Andrew Lang

Thinking I was on top of the world, I married young, at 17. (I do not recommend it.) Remember, I was adapting to my surroundings. Living in Mexico, having a job, and earning enough money to live, marriage seemed like the right thing at that time. Maybe it was in the water—I'm not sure? I was married. I learned really fast that a single teenager with no responsibilities didn't need much to "survive," but when I had a wife and bills, the money I earned in Mexico was just not enough.

Returning to the United States allowed me to set my sights high and my goals even higher. The U.S. is the place where anyone can be anything and everything. I came back to my birthplace, and there was so much potential everywhere! I brought $2 in my pocket, and a do-or-die mentality.

At first, I had a few different jobs where I excelled in every single one, then after I acquired a few startup businesses throughout the years, I flipped for profits along the way. Some were big ones and some were not so great, but every single one was a life lesson learned straight from the streets. My very own hustle code was being written. I became successful the day I realized that losing wasn't an option.

I set my sights high and went for it. Anything I touched for the next 10 years turned to gold, except my first marriage, which lasted about the same length of time. Not letting anything hold me back, I kept pushing forward without looking back at all.

> "You'll never know where you're going, unless you know where you've been."
> —Eddie B.

As much as I would like to fill this book with a million success stories about how I became a millionaire in one year, working two to six hours per week while on the beach drinking margaritas, it's not going to happen! I've been busting my ass daily since I was 13 years old—working, perfecting, and failing. I've made a lot of money, and I've lost a lot of money. I've made many friends and a few enemies along the way. And nothing will give you a better return on investment (ROI) than hard work and dedication.

Accepting your failures and owning them is the best advice I can give you. Owning that my first marriage failed, and ended in divorce, allowed me to learn that life moves on with you or without you. Don't get me wrong, "I am successful!" I became successful the day I realized that losing wasn't an option.

"Success," to me, is a state of mind You must look deep into your personal life, further than you think. For some of us, it's because of the need to survive, for others, it's because they grew up poor, or because they would get beaten as kid, or because they were an orphan, or because they were divorced and a single mother of four children!

Whatever that reason is, find it as fast as possible. Make the choice and act on it right away. And, yes, anyone can do it. So can you. There are not many things in my life that I regret, because I even learned from my fails. As a matter of fact, I thank all my fails for making me the person I am today.

> **"You can't ever taste real success, until you've tasted real failure"**
> —Eddie B.

After returning to the United States, married and with my son on the way, I decided that I would grow myself to become the biggest person I could. My first job, like most of you, was at a fast-food restaurant (Carl's Jr.). I had just had my seventeenth birthday, and I was on a mission to accomplish it all. As I worked extremely hard, long hours, and extra shifts, I noticed everyone around me. All the kids my age were working the minimum they could possibly work, to get a few bucks in their pockets.

I clearly remember them counting down the clock to go to a party, the beach, or a weekend car show. All they needed was a few hundred dollars, because they needed a new car stereo system in their car. However, I was soon buying diapers and paying rent. But I was happy! I had my son! He was born in 1995. (I was only 17.) The only thing on my mind was making him the happiest kid around.

After a short one year of working at that fast-food place, I was promoted to assistant store manager. I was so young that special approval had to be obtained from the corporate office to promote someone as young as I was then. The day I turned 18, I was a manager. However, I wanted more. I wanted bigger!

> "When you focus on your 'why,' you will soon discover your 'how.'"
> —Eddie B.

I learned about a job opening at a high-end jewelry store in Anaheim, California, looking for salespeople. I applied and got that job! It was the best/worst on-the-job training anyone will ever have! My training consisted of certain tactics that now I know were borderline illegal. What I mean was this, the owner of this establishment was so strict that he would curse at us while training and even send us home for two days without pay, if we made one mistake.

I will never forget my first day on the job. I was supposed to arrive in a three-piece suit. I remember shopping for two days for the right suit, and I thought I was ready. I arrived at work looking as fly as possible, smelling as clean as a bar of Dove soap. I walked in, clocked in, and I was on the floor ready.

The owner approached me and looked me up and down. "Let me see your fingernails. Turn around. Go home!"

"Wait... Why?"

"Go home and change that suit jacket!" He said, "Never ever drive your car wearing your suit jacket. It's all wrinkled. It matters what you look like."

I made the round-trip drive in Los Angeles traffic and it took 2.5 hours.

I returned to work and got behind the counter. Soon a customer walked in. I said what most people would say in a retail establishment. "Hello, how may I help you?" Blah, blah, blah, blah... as the owner watched me through a one-way mirror between his office and the sales floor. I soon heard over the public address (PA) system, "Eddie to the office, please."

I learned that saying, "How may I help you?" was a big no-no to that owner. He said to me, "Customers don't come in here because they need help; they come in here to be served,"

I was doing what I thought was a killer sales presentation. Then the unimaginable happened. My next customer came in, and as I was serving her needs, my customer asks, "Can I see that ring please?" I thought I was on fire! My inner head said to me, "Yes, that's the biggest stone in the display case," as I reached in to get the 5.5-carat, diamond ring worth more than $25,000.

I felt a hand on my shoulder and heard a whisper in my ear, "If you ever pull another piece of jewelry out of that case without prior approval, you're fired," as he greeted the customer with a smile. Needless to say, he took over that deal. And for those of you who are wondering, yes, he closed the deal on a 1.5-carat, diamond engagement ring worth $7,000. I witnessed the entire transaction and I must admit I was in love—I was in love with the sales game! I found out what turns me on! I wanted him to teach me everything he did.

Sure enough, for the next year or so, every day he taught everything, from our hand motions, our facial expressions, how we stood, how we held our hands while standing, and even how we breathe during a deal. I came in early and left late every day. There was no social media yet, no Internet. Without modern-day resources available to me at that time, I found myself reading on my lunch break and going to the library on my off day.

I learned about diamonds and precious stones. I did that daily for about a year. Then, I became the store manager! I had my own new store! Remember, at that point I was only 18 years old. I was in charge of more than one million dollars of inventory daily. I always broke sales records. I was on top of my game. I was on fire! I wanted more. I wanted bigger!

> "The only way to do great work is to love what you do."
> —Steve Jobs

At that point, I loved jewelry, gold, and diamonds. I wondered what the largest jewelry store chain was. It's Walmart! Most people don't even imagine Walmart as a jewelry store, but the discount store is all over the world, and it's a staple in every state. So, I applied, and I got the job. I hate to sound cocky, but I changed the way Walmart sold jewelry.

I went in every day with a different mentality than most Walmart employees; I was wearing a three-piece suit! That's right—a three-piece jacket, never worn while driving. I learned at my prior job that shoppers will more likely buy from a professional in the field, therefore, I dressed like one. I was a simple employee, but walking in to work every day, everyone thought I owned that store.

I operated at such high levels that even the department manager was amazed. I "borrowed" a kitchen timer from the housewares department. I set it to go off every 20 minutes or so, and every time it would buzz, I would get on the P.A. System with a promotion in both English and Spanish in my radio voice "Free ar piercing for everyone! Please choose the pair your would like to buy" I always had some type of promotion going on. The customers seemed to like it, because I was making deals! But I know I annoyed the store employees, as they had to listen to me every 20 minutes during the eight hours they were there. I did what others wouldn't do, to separate myself from the masses. I wanted more. I wanted bigger!

> "Today I will do what others won't, so tomorrow I can accomplish what others can't."
> —Jerry Rice

During my short stay at Walmart, I took a small vacation (mandatory). I remember not wanting to take a vacation, because I never had vacation money, but I did. I took a six-hour drive to Las Vegas, Nevada, and played poker for a few days, winning a couple of small Texas Hold'em tournaments. On my drive out of town, I remembered I had about $4,000 left to my name (it was like a million dollars to me at that time), and I saw "the next best thing"—a beautiful, white, 1992 Lincoln Continental, six-passenger limousine. It had a "For Sale" sign on the window. I pulled the driver over in such a fashion that when I think about it now, I wouldn't have stopped if I were him. But the 80-year-old man did.

He wanted $8,000 for that limo. I gave him everything I had—$4,000 cash that day and promised to bring him another $4,000 in seven days! Then, I'm driving back home with no money. I'm broke, scared, confused, and nervous, but I've never been happier! I knew I could do it; I wasn't sure what I was going to do, but I knew I could do it.

I spent the next few days booking future limo rides to come up with money. I also sold just about everything I had, which wasn't much, as I was still short about $2,000. I traded my Acura Integra for my brother's 1990 Oldsmobile. I called the old man and made a second deal with him. My balance was $4,000, and I only had $2,000. I agreed to pay him $2,000 cash and my only mode of transportation, my Oldsmobile.

He said, "Yes!" So, I drove my car back to Vegas, picked up my limo, and drove back. I had no sleep, no Money, and no idea how, but I knew it was going to work! I couldn't sleep, so I parked that limo in my driveway. I printed my own flyers and business cards at home—black-and-white ink on colored paper—and passed them out like they were candy.

I remember parking outside of various high schools, passing out cards and flyers on my days off. I was still working at Walmart jewelry department. As a matter of fact, I would drive that limo to work daily, and I would park it as far as possible from the entrance of the store with flyers stuck to the window. When I would come out after work, they were all gone! People would get the flyers off the car because my cellphone and pager started to ring. Honestly, my pager and cellphone would ring so much, people thought I was dealing drugs.

It was a secret that I had a limo at work. I didn't want to get fired or get in trouble. I was only three months into it, and I was already trying to get my second limo. With a small loan from my sister in law, I paid cash for my second limo, and I finally realized that there was no stopping me. I grew the business to four limos in my driveway, until the city came to me with an order to impound my cars if I didn't move them. So, I did.

I got an old, beat-up, standalone building and renovated it—the place didn't even have closed-in garages, only carports. I converted all of them to fully enclosed garages to house my limos. I grew that business to six, 10-passenger limos and one, 20-passenger Lincoln Navigator. I was 20 years old when I bought that first limo for $8,000 cash. Then at 23 I bought my first Navigator for $60,000. I was on top of the world! At least I felt that way, you can only imagine what a 21-year-old kid making more than $5,000 per weekend would live like.

I built the business from scratch in what seemed like overnight, and I also lost it in what seemed like overnight. I had the great idea of selling it. I found a "buyer" (thief) at $125,000 cash. We made the deal, and he offered me a $15,000 cash deposit in late May. I was to return in July to pick up the balance of $110,000. When I returned in July to pick up my money, I realized that he never had any intention of paying me any more money at all. After court battles, lawsuits, and attorney fees, I have never been able collected a penny from that deal. I was forced to repossess all the cars and sell them wholesale, just to recuperate some of the money I lost. It was the biggest financial gain and loss of my life that happened in my early 20s. I wanted more. I wanted bigger!

> "Life's not about how hard of a hit you can give... it's about how many you can take, and still keep moving forward."
> —Sylvester Stallone, *Rocky Balboa*

I was fearless. I was not about to let that thief who stole my limo company win. I was put on this earth to win. I decided to open a nightclub/restaurant with little to no money (funded primarily by playing poker daily). I found a closed nightclub, and in retrospect that building should have been burned to the ground. I remodeled for days, weeks, then months. I redid everything.

In 2003, I opened the "Copacabana Night Club and Restaurant, and upscale salsa club. I was 23–24 years old. I opened it with a temporary dance permit and fought with the city for three years. After tens of thousands of dollars and countless appeals, I never won that battle, so I decided to sell the place to a restaurant owner. Thirteen years later, all my work is still visible. From the new palm trees to the new blacktop driveway, and even the handicap parking stall—I put all that in.

My entire life, I've adapted to my surroundings. I've learned to make something out of nothing, live, and learn. I love fixing broken businesses, For the following 10 years, I opened/flipped at least eight new start-ups, and I've learned from every single one. Six cellphone stores, a furniture store, an all-male hair salon, a sales consultant business, a candy bouquet franchise, a limousine service, and a nightclub/restaurant, just to name a few. And I have been a consultant to at least 10 businesses, still in operation today. One of my future business will be an upscale cigar, blues bar in Mexico.

I don't come from a family with money. I've never had a loan from my parents. I don't have some type of secret security fund! Every single situation I've been involved with has been mostly by myself and, in a few instances, partnerships with close friends or brothers. I mostly enjoy the process of making something out of nothing, much like an artist with a black canvas. I love the adrenaline. I love the ups and down and the challenges that come from opening a new business.

I always have my eyes open, I always ask, "What is next?" Today, I do more self-employed, sales consultant work. I help businesses, which are low in the sales department, market and sell more products. I create and implement latest sales practices and marketing ideas to stay up with this ever-changing sales world.

But most of all I love helping people accomplish more and make more of whatever they want to make more of. I find it rewarding to teach new salespeople (or old ones) who want to learn new ways. I'm proud to have been involved in many businesses today that are still going strong.

Here are some words about me from people I've been able to help.

> For over three years, Eddie has helped me expand my business by teaching me how to efficiently use my time. He's helped to produce quality-based services to my customers. Eddie taught me the concept of value, which was the turning point for my business and I couldn't be happier. My business has literally doubled in size since I've followed Eddie's ideas and practices.
> —Pricilla A., Southern California Day Care

> Eddie was my first employer at the age of 14 at a cellphone store in Las Vegas, Nevada. I remember when he told me, "Richie Rich, I am going to teach you how to sell, and if you learn how to sell you will never struggle nor die of hunger." And he was damn right! At the age of 14, I was making $600–1,000 a week selling cellphones! I quickly became his top sales associate. Eddie became my mentor, and 12 years later I still learn from him every day. Everything he taught me about sales changed my life. I have never struggled to make an income, even if I'm not rich and wealthy or a millionaire. My knowledge of sales that I have learned from Eddie I apply every day. I now can pass on the

knowledge. I get to train and coach my employees with his sales training tips every day! He always told me to make a customer into a client with five simple, questions used in sales all over the world everyday: Who? What? Where? When? Why? Who are you? What are you in need of? When are you looking to make this happen? What are you shopping for? What can we talk about? Where did you hear about me or the business? When's the best time to reach out to you? And one of the most important facts I learned from Ed is, "Don't be afraid of rejection!" To this day, I still learn from Eddie, and I'm thankful I got to meet him and be his friend for the past 12 years and more to come! He's like family now!
—Richard M., Auto Zone Management

No matter how many good things I tell you I've learned and applied from Eddie, it will never do it true justice. He has changed my life for the better. I was broke. No job. No family, and I slept on my mom's couch. When he met me, he treated me like I was a millionaire. He offered me a job as a sales consultant in his cellphone store. I had never sold a thing in my life. I was afraid of rejection. He told me that if listened to his training, I would quickly become a top producer. After only two months, I made it to first place, and I stayed there for many months and even years. I became first place in something for the first time in my life. I couldn't believe I was better in sales than all the other

bilingual, long-time, employees currently working at that store, especially because that store was in a primarily Hispanic neighborhood, and I am a 22-year-old black man, not bilingual. Now I'm enrolled in school, taking Spanish as my second language. I'm the store manager. Eddie, you saved my life. Thanks
—Lamont B., Cricket Wireless

Growing up without a father was tough, my mother worked two to three jobs just to keep food on the table. I was roaming the streets, like most 16 year olds. As fate were to have it, I often wandered into my local Walmart store, and I often stopped to talk to one of the managers at that time. Who was going to know that Eddie was soon going to become my friend, mentor, and I now consider him as part of my family. He offered me a job in the pet department, stocking merchandise. I clearly remember that job. I hated it, but every day I got a chance to talk to Eddie, and he motivated me to keep pushing. After many years, we stayed in contact, as I saw many of my friends amount to nothing or in gangs, drugs, or in jail. I did just like Eddie told me and became a licensed Realtor. I thought I was on top of the world, but he kept on pushing me, and I kept on listening. Now I'm also a licensed broker in California. Statistics show that a Hispanic male growing up without a father and living the life I lived is 80 percent more likely to end up in jail or dead by the age of 22. I'm

not a statistic. I'm a successful real estate broker, owner, Realtor, and entrepreneur.
—Juan B., Real Estate Broker/Owner/Realtor

I'm a big believer that no matter what your situation in life, your race, your gender or even the level of education you have, you too can become whatever you want to become, if you truly desire it. If you put your soul into finding "what turns you on," you will become successful. I guarantee it! Even though I might not know you, and you might not know me, if there is ever anything I can do for you, please reach out to me. I'll be more than happy to help you accomplish your goals.

Your success will more than likely not be your first move or even your fifth move. More than likely, your success will be compiled of many failures. So, my best advice that I can give you is this.

"Hurry up and fail many times, so you can hurry up and win."
—Eddie B.

This chapter is dedicated to my father, Anthony Peter Bordens (April 4, 1935–September 16, 1988), who lost his life to make sure I made my own way. I know he has been with me every single step of the way. Thanks Pops. P.S. I'll make you proud.

Edward Bordens is a Sales Professional. He excels in this profession due to his passion for overcoming objections. Edward has been in the Sales industry for over 25 years. Edward has gained experience from his travels Internationally & throughout the United States. Most of you may know Edward from Grant Cardone's "Whatever It Takes" reality TV show. He appeared in Season 1, competing against other sales professions from all over the country and won 1st place. He also received Top Outside Sales Agent award, placing him into the Presidents Club for top credit card processing company. Selling over 2 million+ dollars of inventory within a year also set a new self-standard for Edward. Edward continues to mentor many young aspiring individuals in both their personal and professional lives. To which almost all of them are now in high demand positions or successfully operating their own businesses. Edward never hesitates to educate or guide anyone who asks of his help. Edward is self-employed as a Sales Consultant & in addition to that holds the title of Regional Sales Director for a reputable, leading, outdoor patio furniture manufacturer company and is working diligently with investors to further expand the company into new markets.

TURNING TRAGEDY INTO TRIUMPH

EDGAR HURTADO

It sounds crazy, but the fact that my grandfather was shot and murdered in front of my five-year-old mother somehow has, in a weird way, made me the man I am today… Stay tuned and I'll connect the dots for you. Let me continue.

MY TWO ROCKS AND THREE REASONS

Before anything, I thank God for giving me the vision to see the opportunities that have come my way.

Also, there would be no Edgar Hurtado without my parents, Trinidad and Yolanda Hurtado. They were, and continue to be, my support through all the good times and the bad times. They have guided me, taught me, instilled great values and a work ethic in me, and beat my ass from time to time, but I deserved it. What can I say? We're Mexican.

My children (Priscilla, Giovanni, and Arianna Hurtado) are and will always be my **why**. I work really hard to provide for them, not just financially but also in the development of their minds and choices. I also want them to know that in life, nothing comes easy. It takes hard work to achieve any goal. They need to appreciate and enjoy the journey as well as the result. I truly love my kids and I am very proud of them. They have grown to be amazing young adults.

Finally, I would like to acknowledge the many people who have had an impact on my life in some sort of way. You know the saying, "It takes a village to raise a child." Trust me, it took two villages to raise me.

Para mis padres: les quiero dar las gracias por todo lo que han hecho por mi. Sin ustedes no estuviera donde estoy ahorita. Ya haciendo Padre yo entiendo todos los sacrificios que han hecho para mi hermana y yo. Yo se que habien tiempos que fueron muy dificiles para nuestra familia, pero trabajaron muy duro para sacar nos por adelante. Gracias por todos las lecciones de la vida. Yo se que no fui el perfecto hijo y que cause muchas problemas, pero siempre estuvieron alli para no dejarme caller muy abajo. Por todo esto les doy las gracias.

Ok, enough with the acknowledgments.

THE ORIGINAL HUSTLERS

Amarate los huevos, apreitate el cinturon y cumple. —My Loving Mother

Tu eres como un cerillo, te aprendes y luego te apagas muy pronto.
Mejor enfocate en algo y ponte a trabajar cabron.
—My Caring Father

My name is Edgar Hurtado. These two phrases are from my parents. My parents told it like it was and never sugarcoated anything. They had many such phrases they told me as I was growing up. As any normal child would do, I would never pay any attention to them or what they meant. Now, as I am older, I have realized that my Mexican-born parents knew all the secrets to success, and all I had to do was just listen to them. I'll get back to you in another book about all the success lessons taught to me by my crazy Mexican parents. (I promise the book will be enlightening and funny.)

In this book, I'm going to focus on the two statements that my parents used to tell me, which have helped me achieve some type of success and have guided me through tough times and put me in positions to be successful. I believe these statements are the foundation to having true leadership habits.

But first, let me tell you about my parents. Both my parents are from a small town near Guadalajara, Mexico, called Jalostotitlan Jalisco, and damn are they proud to be from there. Every summer, we used to vacation there, so I could know my roots, according to my parents. We went for Carnaval and Las Fiestas.

At an early age, my father, Trinidad Hurtado, the oldest of 13, had to go to work to help provide for the rest of the family. Holy crap, can you imagine feeding 13 kids? Yes, I said 13—no typo here. I guess Grandpa didn't believe in television or watching novelas. My father developed great work skills and habits as a child, which he always tried to instill in me (the original hustler). From what I saw growing up, he was always on time. Time management is his thing. I still remember him telling me, "If you're ten minutes early to work, *you are late*!"

He had great respect for his job and the people he worked for and with. My father developed many relationships and work opportunities because of his work ethic. My father always, I mean always, provided for his family. Even if he had to work two or three jobs. (Talk about hustling—true example here.) We never needed for anything. My dad is the cool guy. The one people want to be around at the parties. He loves life. He is a simple man.

My mother, on the other hand, is a completely different story. Yolanda Hurtado is a tough woman. My mother is the second youngest of seven children, which is still a lot of kids in one family in today's times, but my dad's family still takes the gold medal in this event. You see, I believe it was my mother's circumstances that made her who she is. Let me tell you my beliefs.

My mother's father (my grandfather) was murdered coming out of his house while carrying my mother in his arms. She witnessed her father get gunned down by someone close to the family over a land dispute that my grandfather had refused to sell at an early age. I'm sure that was such a traumatic moment in her life. This is when the legend of Yolanda Hurtado started.

You have to understand that after the murder, it was up to my grandmother and all the daughters to protect and provide. It was all women in the household. Let me tell you that all my aunts are some tough-ass women. I mean really tough, afraid-of-nothing type women.

Back to my mother—I'll give you the short version. My mother became a smart, savvy business woman and still is today. She is the one who keeps the house in order from bills to finances to making dinner every night (a true wonder woman). On top of all this, she worked her whole life. How she did all this, only God knows (another hustler). She is huge on doing what you say you are going to do. Her word is golden, and so should yours be, according to her. My mother has many amazing qualities that society believes is not normal for a typical woman (more on the legend of my mother in my next book). Above all, one thing for sure, my mother does not ever let anyone fuck with her.

Why do I tell you about my parents and who they are? The reason is that without them and the qualities they possess, there would be no Edgar Hurtado. I believe when it comes to me, I got both of my parent's qualities. I believe I have a good personality and I enjoy having fun as well as developing good relationships with people. I believe I am a hard worker (although there is always room for improvement). I believe that my parents raised a sharp and honest man who has learned the hustle code. The key to all success is in the hustle.

THE BIRTH OF A HUSTLER

THE REAL EARLY DAYS

I still can recall the exact moment when I got bit by the entrepreneurial bug. Even though I didn't know what business or entrepreneurship was, I sure did know what *money* was and the *power* it provided. It all started in first grade in Miss Orlans class. I was a kid who liked to daydream and doodle a lot. I would draw and color pictures of such things as Snoopy, Hello Kitty, and such popular things during those days. The other students loved them and would always ask me to draw them a picture. Bingo! (Soooooo, what you are saying is that you like what I'm drawing.) I became in demand in the first grade.

I started hustling pictures of Snoopy, Garfield, and Hello Kitty for a nominal fee—usually 5 or 10 cents. (Hey! I know it's not that much, but it was a start and it became my seed money.) I started slinging drawings on a daily. The thing I learned early on is that if the hustle is for you, then you automatically become addicted. Business and the hustle became my drug, and I was always looking for the next hit.

STILL THE EARLY DAYS

I had now gotten older (approximately 8) and too cool to hustle my previous product of drawings, so I took my seed money and started a new business. I became the candy man. Yes, you heard it right—I started to hustle candy. I would get up extra early in the morning and run to Rockview Dairy near my house to purchase candy. Then I would run back to school, so I wouldn't be late and be undetected.

My usual product would consist of a bunch of different-flavored Now and Later candy. (This was my highest return on investment.) I would also get other candy that had single pieces, so I could sell individual pieces. For example, Now and Later candy was 10 cents at the time for 10 pieces. I would then sell the 10 pieces individually for 5 cents. Talk about great instant returns—cha-ching! I was hooked.

I also started to notice the other side of success. There was something I realized. I was becoming popular, and I was becoming *the man* in second grade. With success, comes much responsibility. People started to follow me and look up to me. Also, I learned to beware of leeches, who were only around to suck me dry, just because I had experienced some success and put change in my pocket (in this case, literally). These are more of the lessons I learned in my early stages of entrepreneurship.

THE PAPER ROUTE HUSTLE

I now was becoming a full-fledge baller. I had graduated from drawings and candy to starting my empire in the paper route business. At nine years of age, I got a job with my local neighborhood newspaper, *Evening Outlook*. I had approximately 70 homes I delivered to each day after school. I was making $100–120 a month. Since I was already a seasoned businessman at nine years of age, I began to come up with a way to expand the Hurtado empire. I decided to get three more paper routes in the neighborhood. You see, I've never been afraid of hard work, not even when I was a youngster.

I did all four routes for a while, but it was taxing on me and took too much time. So, I began to think, *There have to be other kids in the neighborhood who like money and hard work like I do.* I started asking around, and, in no time, I recruited my first employees. I was a *boss* at the age of ten. I owned the routes, so I was able to pay out a fair salary for the job rendered. I paid out three kids (employees) $75 per month. They loved that I had given them an opportunity to make some money, and I loved the fact that I was making money without working.

At this moment of my entrepreneurial journey, I learned two valuable lessons. First, stop trading time for dollars. I was doing four paper routes and not enjoying the fruits of my labor. Second, it's better to have 1 percent of 100 people's efforts, than 100 percent of my own.

You see, I was making $25–45 per route without even working. Also, if something had happened to me, my income stream would have stopped. I realized I needed a good team to expand and grow. In order to grow any business, you need good loyal people who see your vision and will support you. They need to be people who will speak up when needed. You don't need "yes" men. At any early age, I found out that good personal relationships with your team is important for growth. This goes hand in hand with your hustle savvy.

THE FALL OF A HUSTLER

THE CRASH OF A PAPER ROUTE EMPIRE

Everything was going smoothly, but I wanted more, faster. The dollars were coming in monthly (all $400–500 of them), but I wanted more, lots more. So, I went back to the drawing board to expand the Hurtado empire. I thought for days and days until it finally hit me. I knew that over my illustrious business career, at the ripe old age of eleven, I had developed good speaking skills (I call it the gift of gab) that I could put to use. I decided to go door to door to all the customers and strike a deal with them—a deal they couldn't refuse.

I asked them, "If I continue to deliver the paper to you every evening, would you pay me instead of the *Evening Outlook?*" I also offered a discount. It was hard for them to refuse my offer. I was a cute, little, Mexican kid who grew up in the neighborhood trying to survive, so they thought. What they didn't realize was that this was all part of my scam. I had the customers cancel their service.

You see I wasn't being driven by purpose or passion anymore. I was driven by *greed*. So, my master plan was in full effect. The customers were paying about $10–15 per month, and that was all mine now. I had my employees onboard. They even got a pay increase. I think at that time I had approximately 150–170 customers among all four routes. You might be wondering how a snotty-nose kid built this machine. Well, here is your answer. Actually, it was easy.

There were newspaper stands everywhere in town, with approximately 30–50 papers in them. Every day, after school, I would ride my bike to about four or five newspaper stands and put in one quarter and *wham*, I was in pocket. I was in the game, ready to hustle some newspapers. It cost me about $1.00–1.50 every day to play. My trusted employees were now part of the team. They were my loyal soldiers who benefited from my success.

Imagine 10–11 year olds making $2,000 a month. Dang, we were now celebrities in our hood. We had all the new games for the Atari 2600, wore the best Vans (you know the checkered shoes), had fresh OP shorts on. We were *ballers*. Every Saturday, we would go to Westworld arcade to blow our money and show off. I really think that when our crew walked in to the arcade, everything went to slow motion. I compare it to *The Wolf of Wall Street*. I was the Jordan Belfort of paper routes. One problem though, my vision was cloudy, and I was driven by greed, instead of a higher purpose.

I wasn't enjoying the journey anymore. I wanted the results and fast. After a short while, the newspaper company caught on and busted me. They wanted to press charges. I remember I was shitting bricks. I wasn't scared about the police. I was terrified about what my mother was going to do to me. I hope you haven't forgot about my mother. She was, and still is, one bad-ass woman who doesn't play. I was in a shit load of trouble. It was going to be more than the dreaded *chancla* this time. It was time for the heavy artillery. It was time for the *cinto* (the belt). Damn, I hated that thing. That shit hurts.

You see, my mother is extremely honorable. She believes in the hustle and everything about it, but stealing is a big no-no. She always would tell me to work hard and earn everything, so no one could talk shit about me. If it's worth having, you have to love the struggle to get it. (El trabajo es lo bonito de la vida. Tenemos que sufri par apreciar. I didn't want to struggle.) I didn't get this. Anyway, I was banned for life at hustling newspapers. I was devastated. I had saved enough money that made me feel better about myself, but the glitz and glamour was all gone. I remember thinking, *Dang, now what?* I wanted that feeling back of being the man. Trust me, that's a good feeling. I don't care what anyone says!! Time to regroup.

THE IDLE YEARS

During my teens, I did what most teenagers do. I went to high school, hung out with friends, and had odd jobs. I basically just did the norm. I did what society tells us to do. Get your high school diploma, go to college, get a job, get married, have kids, and die. Yes, I said *die*. Hell no, not me! Look, there is nothing wrong with working and sacrificing. I just always believed in my soul I was put here for bigger and better things. *We all are.*

We get one chance at this thing called life. There are no do-overs, no my bads, no restarts, no dress rehearsal, and no nothing. *It's one take, one chance.* That's it. So, make the best of it. Sorry about the rant. I get really passionate about this subject.

Anyway, I wanted more, not just financially, but mentally and spiritually. Remember I was bit early with the business bug. I was always looking for the next thing. Studying people, reading books, learning, and taking everything in that I could. I craved and needed knowledge.

THE I ALMOST MADE IT HUSTLE

Right out of college, I was itching for the next master plan—the next business. I got into selling Chinese products of all kinds in Mexico. I started out with toys and other seasonal things. This was at the beginning of NAFTA, when Chinese products were being taxed up the yin yang in Mexico. I had a close hookup, though, who would cross all my merchandise at a flat fee (you know, la mordida).

I started this business, just by door knocking in certain cities in Mexico. I would walk into stores and ask the owners, "If I can sell you this product landed in Mexico at the same price you are paying for it in Los Angeles, would you buy from me?" Another offer they couldn't refuse. No risk to them at all. One by one, I started getting customers. My business grew so big, so fast, that I lost control. My parents kept warning me: no albarques mucho, mejor despacio pero seguro.

I got to the point where I had a 25,000-square foot warehouse in Los Angeles on Esperanza Street. Money was flowing, but there were no systems or structure in place. My business was like the Wild West. It didn't matter, so I thought. I was trying to push out so much product that it led to the biggest mistake I could make. I started to give credit in Mexico.

I figured if someone was buying $50K of product a month, what if I gave them credit of $100K payable in 30–60 days? I was going to be rich. Nope—not at all. The opposite happened. I lost everything and had to get help from my parents. I was sued for the remainder of my $6,000-a-month lease. It was all bad. What happened? Well, here goes.

I had lots of money on rotating credit, and the Mexican economy crashed. Just like that, I hit rock bottom once again. The peso was trading at 4.5 to the dollar, and, when the economy tanked, it shot to about 15 pesos to the dollar. So, if someone owed me $100K, they now owed me nearly $400K, because of the money conversion. I sold my product in dollars, but my customers sold in pesos. Done!!! Kiss the baby goodnight. (There is a lot more to this story, but I gave you the short version.)

So, it was back to the drawing board. One thing for sure, I wasn't done yet, not even close. I would fall down four times, but get up five times.

THE JOURNEY OF A HUSTLER

MY PRESENT HUSTLE

During the past decade or so, I have been involved in many different businesses. They ranged from cell phone accessories, selling cars, selling products to 99 cent stores, multi-level marketing (**MLM**), and many other things. I had some success in all of them, but not sustainable success. Then I found the holy grail, the thing I love the most next to my family—real estate! I have always dabbled in real estate, but at a small level. Also, my parents have bought and sold several properties. They are in the long-term residual income part of real estate. They have several buy-and-hold properties that they collect rent on monthly.

I don't say any of this to brag, although I am proud of what they have accomplished in this great country. I say this to show you that if a young Mexican couple, recently married and naïve to this country with a language barrier (and by language barrier I mean "no speaky de English at all"), can make it, anyone can. There are no excuses. Excuses only satisfy the people who make them. No one cares how you feel. Get out there and put in the work.

Someone once said, "If you find what you truly love or are passionate about, you'll never work a day in your life." I think I have found my passion. I believe that I'm actually good at what I do, but I'm still getting better. I will do this until the day I die. It's fun for me and it's not work. It's passion. Now, I have a new vision and purpose, along with a great team of cofounders.

We want to educate the masses on how anyone can achieve wealth through real estate. I'm not talking about your late-night scammy guru bullshit. We want to teach people real deals by real people. Show them through hard work and persistence they too can have great success in real estate. We want to start a real estate revolution.

Lastly, I would like to tell you one of my secrets to success. Always strive for the result you want, but enjoy the journey. If you are a true hustler, there will never be no destination, only the journey. You'll never stop the hustle, until you are looking up at the church ceiling and witnessing people saying great things about you, talking about the legacy you left behind. That's when this amazing rollercoaster of a journey will be finally over.

Learn to enjoy all the good and bad of your personal journey!

BONUS MATERIAL

This book is called *The Hustle Code.* I'm going to share the biggest secret to the code. Please don't share it with anyone. It's a deep secret of only the truly successful. Ok, ready? Here it goes. It's called *hard work,* and it includes long hours, sleepless nights, consistency, and a no-quit attitude. Are you surprised there are no magic pills, no algorithms, and no short cuts? It's all hard work. Even motivation is somewhat bullshit. That's only temporary. If you want to be successful, then get off your ass and get to work. There are no short cuts, only hard work. It can take you years to become an overnight success.

NOTES TO TAKE WITH YOU

- You need to become addicted to the hustle.
- With success, comes much responsibility.
- Beware of leeches.

- Stop trading time for dollars.
- It's better to have 1 percent of 100 people's efforts, than 100 percent of your own.
- Build a team for growth.
- Develop good personal relationships.
- Be driven by purpose and passion, not greed.
- Enjoy the journey more than the results.
- You only get one chance at this thing called life.
- No albarques mucho, mejor despacio pero seguro.
- Fall down four times. Get up five times. Never quit!
- Excuses only satisfy the people who make them. No one gives a shit about your feelings.
- Find what you are truly passionate about.
- It will take you years to become an overnight success.
- Live the life you dream of, and make sure you leave a footprint.

> "You can never leave footprints that last if you are always walking on tiptoe."
> —Leymah Gbowee

Do you believe you were born to just pay bills and die, to never experience anything in life? I sure don't. Life is something that we only get one chance at it. There are no redos or mulligans. There are no my bads, I was just kidding. Like the Eminem song, "Lose Yourself," states,

"Look, if you had one shot, or one opportunity

to seize everything you ever wanted, in one moment

Would you capture it or just let it slip?"

I am asking you today to follow your dreams now. Make them a priority. Life is short and you will wake up one day and wonder what happened. Capture this life you were blessed with, and don't let it slip away. You are more than capable. It only takes you to make that decision.

TIPS ON CREATING FOOTPRINTS IN THIS LIFE

Your funeral—think with the end in mind. Picture your funeral (I know it sounds morbid, but follow me). What are people saying about you? What accomplishments are they talking about? What are your loved ones (kids, family members, coworkers, people you influenced) saying about you? What legacy (your footprint on this life) did you leave? After you picture this, let's reverse engineer it. Let's start living your life with those end goals in mind. Set up daily, monthly, yearly goals to get to that footprint you will be leaving.

Know what you want first—have clear and concise goals in all areas of your life—financial, health, relationships, spiritual, etc. This is important to write out. If you don't have a clear destination to where you want to go, someone else might steer you off your true path and onto their path. Know what you want and where you are going.

Put in the work—no one said it was going to be easy. All great things take hard work. The best and most successful people have never become overnight successes. It can take several years, even decades, to become an overnight success. Most people just see the results but not the journey with all the bumps and bruises that you incurred. There are no shortcuts to this game called life, there is only hard work. Fall in love with the process, not the results. Put in the work in all important areas of your life.

Education—read more, take courses, find a mentor, and listen to podcasts.

Health—start working out, eat right, and see your doctor.

Relationships—have a date night with your loved one, block out time for your children, call your parents, take your coworkers or employees out, and call people on their birthdays. There is so much you can do to cultivate and grow in this area.

Financial—start saving more money, make more money, learn about investing and what best serves you, and get out of debt.

Spiritual—find your true self, really understand where you are and where you want to be, get closer to whatever you believe in spiritually, and go out in nature alone (it can be a spiritual experience). This is your personal journey!

Contribution—always pay it forward. Mentor someone, donate money to a good charity, donate your time, and give when it's unexpected. Help those who can't help themselves. This can be done several ways: time, mentorship, lending an ear, monetary, and other opportunities.

Celebrate your success—it always feels good to accomplish something, so when that happens, reward yourself. When you set goals, set rewards alongside them. When that goal is accomplished, then reward yourself for the great job you did to achieve the goal. For example, if you lose 10 pounds, go get yourself a new outfit or a pair of running shoes. Always be striving for more.

Remember, there will never be no final destination, there is only the journey.

We are all special. We all have something to contribute in life. We all have a major footprint to leave behind. We just have to search and be true to ourselves and find out what that is. Once found, we have to get on that path or journey that will lead us to success and to the thousands of people at our funeral saying what a great person you were. You did great things. You left a legacy.

So, I say to you once again, "Look, if you had one shot or one opportunity to seize everything you ever wanted in one moment?"

Edgar Hurtado CEO of Pure Passion Properties

Has a true passion for real estate investing. Edgar has become a great developer as well as a great planner to see projects become reality. Edgar considers building as an art that needs to be taken seriously and thought out.

Edgar was born and raised in Los Angeles and is also a strong believer in education. He received a bachelor's degree in accounting and a master's degree in education and has been involved in the development of inner city at risk students for twenty plus years. Edgar runs the daily operations of a non-public school in Los Angeles and loves to guide and mentor the less fortunate students. He shows them that there are options in life. It only takes a decision to change the direction of their life.

Today Edgar combines his expertise in education and real estate to create several win/win situations in real estate investing. It is his passion to introduce as many people he can in real estate so they can create wealth.

Edgar Hurtado wants to help as many people as he can whichever way he can so he can leave a legacy.

HARD WORK BEATS TALENT

RAFAEL PALOMINO

Growing up around the ag fields of Northern California's San Joaquin Valley, I spent countless afternoons with my father and my brothers, lending a hand, talking, and being taught the lessons of the land, the people, and the water. We would challenge one another with discussions about history and current events, and we'd resolve our arguments with references to an unspoken code of morals and standards, which we took as a form of ancient family principals. We'd often remind ourselves that either right or wrong, you must always be willing to stand up, and go all in, for what you believe in. We knew that second-guessing would only lead us down a path of misery and regret and that without morals and standards, chaos rules.

Never knowing exactly how they managed, my parents somehow throughout the years endured the long and strenuous process of successfully bringing all our family members and their children to this country legally, offering them an opportunity to get ahead. There were times where I'd give up my room and bunk on the screened porch all summer long. My bedroom was given to some traveling cousin, uncle, or grandma.

With my parents' encouragement, before I was twenty-five years old, I had sponsored five families to legally stay in the United States. They were some of the hardest working people I had ever known. Today they are successful entrepreneurs, business people, and pillars in their communities.

This was just one example of the values my parents instilled in all their children. My parents would say, "When something is the right thing to do, and if it is important enough, there is always a way."

They realized that with higher consciousness comes understanding. And just as desperation breeds innovation, I grew up watching business and sales savvy transform not only our entire family structure, but also our outlook and enjoyment of the journey thus far.

Looking back, I can say I reached the stage of my life I'm in today because they worked hard and stayed humble. Today I am a grandfather, a spouse, and a proud proclaimer of freedom because of applying passion, ambition, and purpose in any meaningful thing I do. Doing so, I create a culture that reflects these qualities anywhere I spend any significant amount of time. This has been my legacy, and it has followed me all the years of my life.

My leadership strengths came early in the form of initiative and ideas and the power to convey those ideas effectively and with passion. Realizing this, I shook up my world by creating experiences most don't have the courage to find. From an early age, I became good at creating and navigating through hypersituations.

As you can imagine, growing up this sometimes got out of hand and there would often be consequences. During these consequential downtimes, I would reflect on the patterns, intentions, and emotions leading up to and during these moments. I became a student of people and committed to memory their natural behaviors, reactions, and patterns. This was a skill that would later prove itself useful.

From an early age, I found it easier to focus on my strengths. Being able to read and write in two languages sped things along considerably. Not to mention we were raised Jehovah's Witnesses, so I got a lot of practice preaching at the door and speaking in front of the congregation in both languages. Plus, I would literally read everything I could get my hands on.

My mom, who had worked with and followed business programs including Zig Ziglar, Donald Trump, and Lee Iacocca since the early 1980s, would always leave materials out for us to read. As a kid, I knew that a person who didn't read wasn't much better than a person who couldn't read.

I believe that being well read strengthened my imagination, which made me easier to like. This opened doors and, combined with culture, led my way. I deal with people. And I create my own way.

If I were to recommend a guideline to people looking for the next level or beginning to realize that the properties of the Law of Attraction are essential in the manifestation of a life of reward for service and value, I'd tell them to look around themselves and to find the characters whom they'd like their life to emulate. Then reverse engineer the characters by connecting those attributes to their own, down to this very spot where they are today. The freedoms and blessings around us make this easier than most think.

Like most people starting out, I was drawn to the history of commerce and trade, because it's always shaped our landscape. Knowing my ambitions, my seventh-grade English teacher, while on a field trip to The Haggin Museum in Stockton, California, introduced me to Alex Spanos, a billionaire philanthropist and owner of the Los Angeles Chargers National Football League team. She had told him some about me, and we spent the next few years discussing philosophies in life. He talked to me about business, and we compared cultures. He was impressed with what I knew.

One day Spanos shared that the pressure of being the son of immigrants should push me to get ahead, as it had him; he felt he had to make their sacrifices worth it. A sentiment I already knew something about. He recommended schools to attend and biographies to read. When discussing big business, he'd say to take the emotion out of the deal and to make decisions quickly. We talked about sports and the importance of having a positive culture and vibe. He would say, "You are only as strong as your weakest link."

He admired hard workers and talked about the importance of a workforce. He emphasized how and why to respect them. It was a strong example of attaining high levels of success, while having had humble beginnings. I've always taken this as a gift, and it was natural for me to feel I was on a similar journey. I wondered what I would do if I ever had such influence. Later I would meet successful business entrepreneurs Anthony Batarse and his son, Rudolph.

They would mentor me through a decade in the automobile franchise business, which would later lead me to financial products, real estate, and e-commerce.

The one thing I would say up front about meeting with and having mentors, thought leaders, and coaches is that you still have to make it your own story at the end of the day. Most people want a blueprint, when instead it should be a pattern of work ethic at best. That's why it's so important to do something you love, if you truly want to live your life to the fullest. And to advance effectively, you must first develop as an individual. The more you get comfortable with that notion, the further into the future you can project and manifest your plans and track your progress, not only weekly, monthly, and yearly, but also emotionally.

You want to dig deep into your craft and become as equally good an architect as you are a mason.

Meeting with and having had mentors, combined with a great deal of ambition, positioned me to find new professional environments from which to learn from and grow.

My goal was to learn more about running big business and trade, while taking care of my growing family. The relationships with my mentors, thought leaders, and coaches, would carry me through the ranks of Bank of America, Toyota Motor Corporation, American Honda Finance Corporation, General Motors Acceptance Corporation (GMAC), the California Association of Realtors, and the National Association of Hispanic Real Estate Professionals (NAHREP), where I held a seat on the regional board.

These businesses allowed me to network, which is one of my favorite crafts to perfect, and I became a professional connector of people. The financial gains from these connections would provide funding for innumerable business ventures and startups.

Interestingly, that is where I've had the most fun, brought in the most people, and used it to practice what I've learned from the corporate structure. Big win there. So, when people ask me if I think it's better to have the mindset and skillset of a self-made entrepreneur or the mindset and skillset of someone achieving a corporate title and climbing the corporate ladder, I would say it's better to have the best from both worlds, especially these days.

From the dot-com era of 1995 to the mortgage era of the early 2000s, I've capitalized on my fair share of dramatic moves in the market through networking.

A successful person, after all, knows when and where to push and where to draw from.

And to sleep well at night, how you make your money will be more important than how much you make.

Having a sense of urgency also makes all the difference in the world. It's the reason most people work great under pressure, because people who have their backs against the wall usually perform.

For those of you holding down a job, I'd say to always keep a side hustle. And if you can, make it more than one. The old adage is that it takes seven streams of income to earn a million. The truth today is that when beginning to invest, the more money you have, the more money you'll make.

Successful people fear regret. Unsuccessful people fear failure. Which is why I'd recommend at least starting out as an affiliate to something you love. Trust me, it's less work to win than to lose.

My mentor, Grant Cardone (author, motivational speaker, investor, and sales trainer), says that 76 percent of Americans live paycheck to paycheck, and that becoming a millionaire is joining the new middle class.

Every day at a job felt like wasted time to me. So, I always made sure to have a countdown to a milestone that would trigger my departure, if it wasn't something that I loved.

If I was learning, however, I would try to make the most of it, making sure I was counted among the hardest workers, while at the same time reminding myself that I was only meant to be there long enough to learn what I needed.

As I maneuvered through what I considered my corporate life, I worked to learn, rather than work to earn, something that was instilled in me by my Uncle Salomon, who had been a self-made millionaire since he was young. He taught me that the strength and effectiveness of a successful leader can be measured by the situations in which he feels challenged. To keep from getting complacent, I would make sure to be promoted to different departments and mastered each of their systems.

Toyota, for example, taught me its Japanese system for enticing ingenuity called Kaizen.

I would actually supplement my yearly salary with this incentive by finding opportunities to create new processes and ideas throughout the Toyota logistics division on the West Coast.

I spent several long years there, and my kids got a stay-at-home mom out of the deal.

Most intriguing was that Toyota would reward me with a one time cash bonus equal to the annual savings resulting from my ideas. Not bad. This not only strengthened my creativity; it encouraged ingenuity. And, as you can imagine, I lived outside the box.

Outside the corporate world, I would invest my money into mortgage companies, recording studios, and a merchandise route to Alaska in the early 2000s with my friends.

I think my hustle is what my wife likes most about me. She also thinks these are habits that get stronger with use, as opposed to something that people are born with. Maybe that's why she sticks around.

When picking your life partner, by the way, marry the one who loves the hustle as much as you do or even more. When I met my wife, Mandy, she was working as a political operative, specializing in corporate black ops. She had found her own way to do what she loved—travel and get paid big. Her mindset and focus blew my mind. And although we only dated for a short while before going our separate ways for several years, I thought someday I would come back to find her.

Years later, I did. Her hustle was the same, but her strategies had changed. She had taken what was a fleeting chance on Amazon and reinvented herself by building a business in international trade.

Marrying a powerful and intelligent woman doesn't just double your hustle, it multiplies it. And having a woman by my side who never lets me settle for less has been a blessing.

MINDSET

Just as it is a natural habit for people to follow courage, the same goes for someone who is well informed and has a determined mindset. So, whether it is leading soldiers into battle, like my grandfather, or leading workers into the harvest, like my dad, someone who's fought for and someone who has cared for is also someone who will naturally create self-awareness and courage in others.

As an offspring of confidence, this must be done decisively, unwaveringly, and for the benefit of all. The only way to generate true confidence, however, is through experience. And the best experiences comes from doing what you are most afraid of. In other words, conquer your fears.

Your mindset and skill set also need to be married. Aligning these with the passions of others makes it is easier to convey your messages. I've used this consistently to help thousands break barriers and enhance their positions in social and business arenas. I know that discussing passions generates energy. This energy can be harnessed to create synergy in overlapping interests. And it is this synergy that determines focus, direction, and ultimately results. This can be applied to almost everything in life.

MORNING ROUTINE

First thing in the morning, you want to start with a sense of gratitude. Dedicate yourself in alignment and acknowledgment of all the things that came before you and all the things that lay ahead. Calibrating your sense of gratitude to your sense of acknowledgment will start each day with a sense of duty and better your chances of making it momentous, not to mention influencing everyone around you.

LEARN SOMETHING NEW EVERY DAY

We can always buy the time to build on what we're passionate about. Become an expert at it, and share what you've learned. This will refine your talents.

Again, passion breeds courage. Courage initiates action. Action drives growth, and focus determines velocity. The results will come naturally, if you follow what you are passionate about and invest time in activities that enhance it.

Most people worry about what they're not so good at. In reality, you should accept the fact that it is nearly impossible to have all your skills equally as powerful. Instead focus on what you're best at and become a master. One effective way of balancing this is by continuously surrounding yourself and partnering with people who possess or have the strengths and qualities you're looking to supplement.

VISION

I am convinced that the best possible outcome is always visualized first. A successful person always starts with the end in mind. Start by taking an account of where you are, compared to where you want to be. Map out the milestones. Give yourself a timeframe. And ask yourself, "How bad do I want it?"

Know that the bigger the outcome, the more steps and challenges you might have to face. Be prepared to accept them. Play out the movie in your mind and see how happy it makes you feel. If you really want this change in your life, then have the courage and discipline to make moves of epic proportions.

I learned years ago that every time you take on a meaningful endeavor, you should always look for these three things:

1. What you will take from it.
2. What will you contribute to it.
3. What you will become by it.

Once you have that figured out, only then can you truly give it your all.

When deciding on the best course to get you there, from the beginning, set up and hold yourself to a mission statement or a set of guidelines. This way you'll make all your decisions according to your predetermined principles.

Also, seeing your goals written in your own handwriting has a serious effect on your mind. This by far has given me the fastest results.

If, for any reason, you later find that you're not in love with the path you've chosen, the time it will take to get you there, or the potential outcome, then end it quickly and move on. Check your ego and have the humility to admit and own your mistakes. This will empower you.

Master the art of pivoting while keeping the same end in mind. This is done by accepting and sometimes initiating paradigms in your life. A paradigm is a new way of looking at or thinking about something. This doesn't mean that our principles change; it's our understanding of those principles that eventually changes us. Be ready to pivot at any moment. And when it comes, welcome it. Keep in mind, that often the best outcomes cannot be anticipated, they come from mental agility and the ability to change course quickly. So be decisive.

Luckily for entrepreneurs, there are many paths to take. Pick one of your talents and monetize it. In other words, find something you believe in and that you like and learn how to sell it. It's just like creating a job for yourself. Learn the fundamentals of fulfillment and value exchange, master and then build on them.

An emerging space to keep your eyes on is one that caters to a society driven by instant gratification. To win in this space, all you need to harness and capitalize on is the monetary value of time. This is easier than you think. Look at Uber. It's not a cab company. It is a time company. Uber is valued at more than $60 billion dollars, as of May 2017, because it's in the business of selling you back your time.

Consequently, thousands of people, since the crash of 2007, have discovered that one of the best ways of reaching financial freedom in today's economy is through hard work and entrepreneurship. The failing school systems in the United States have led to entrepreneurship not only becoming fashionable, but an absolute necessity for anyone who wants financial freedom, success, or to make a significant mark in today's society.

Some people are banking on it. One of the most common ways people are entering the entrepreneurial space today is through real estate and e-commerce. I would highly recommend these paths, especially if you can find a community, a mentor, and a system to help you. For more information, I can be reached at raphaelpalomino@gmail.com.

Developing an entrepreneurial mindset has also become a business in itself, with seemingly every moderately successful person directing you to one educational course or another. And the market does what it always does; the best information, tactics, and strategies go to the highest bidder.

There's a lot of money changing hands. I've spoken all across the country throughout the past several years on behalf of the top educational companies, and not since the emergence of NINJA (no income, no job or assets) low-quality, subprime loans in the mortgage industry have I seen something so apparently effective yet disruptive. Now in business, disruption is a good thing—the key, however, is knowing how to convert that disruption to profits.

If you're on the learning side of this curve, I want you to take advantage of this disruption by studying and learning from those who have the most current systems, strategies, and communities that you can plug into. The fastest learning and best strategies are found within these communities. Remember, time is money.

If you want to run one of these successful businesses, position yourself within your sector as an authority with the timeliest information. This doesn't take hours of training or years of experience, it only takes networking and a system to follow.

The difference between a top producer and someone who's average, after all, boils down to the questions they ask.

If you're already in business, ask yourself these questions.

"How much of this could actually help me?"

"Who else needs to hear it?"

"How can I implement processes and ideas?"

Your business will be more efficient and capture market share.

When people reach out to me, one of the first things I suggest is getting involved in bringing value to your space by asking yourself how you could set yourself apart and whose ideas and practices could you join forces with versus just having the mentality of who else you can hire. Be bold and do this with audacity. Remember, the market is always growing.

PURPOSE

To be certain is to have purpose or a "why," which is your reason for doing what you've set out to do. Being passionate about your purpose helps you effect change with a lasting impact. It means to have left things better because you were there; you sparked ideas into fruition, along with your peers, and your sense of contribution carries into future endeavors.

Being reminded of your purpose allows your attitude and behavior to be in harmony with your deepest values and principles. People admire and respect this integrity, especially when your standards and directions are clear. My boy, Gee, from Atlanta recently called and said, "You have a gift," when on the topic of this message. This always reinforces me, and I take into account the work that's been done, along with the work that is being done, to pass on this message. I thank God for allowing me to share in that privilege.

Once you get to this point, it's the journey and sense of growth and accomplishment that should be enough to drive you. You'll know you're on the right path when you begin to like the person you've become.

Here's the thing, you picked up this book for a couple of reasons. Either you knew one of the authors, or you were hoping to find some truths that applied to you.

So, here's a truth: everything you need to succeed, at anything you want to do, is already in you. You just need someone to believe it. Share your ideas with that one person you know will be in your corner and then give it your all.

Because, often, someone who is optimistic stays positive. And recognizing people with a determined purpose will expand your vision. Look for those whose *why* aligns with yours.

To guarantee your success, you must also be emotionally invested in what you're doing. This is the most important part of your *why*. The greater your investment, or the deeper the *why*, the better your chances are.

This is also why sometimes in the beginning, if you don't have a strong enough *why* yet, it is better to work to learn, rather than work to earn. It is not an uncommon story for the most successful people to have started as interns or junior associates. A year or two is time well spent immersing yourself to understand how a great company or organization works in all its functions. You will be much better for the knowledge gained, once you venture out on your own.

For those of you who are ready and are just waiting for a spark, let me be the first to tell you that personal success, like freedom, is an ongoing process. Which is why when you do something that you like repeatedly, you can't help but get good at it. So, don't wait to get started. Your next level starts one step outside your comfort zone.

You also have to believe in people. I mean who else is going to help you? If you know what and where you ultimately want to be, you have to spend as much time as you can with people who are already there. Find people you believe in, and find a way to get close to them and to learn from them. Bring something to the table. The easiest way to do this is by engaging and bringing value to them and also to those closest to them. If the person you are hoping to emulate is someone out of reach, do something bold or persistent to get their attention. My friend, Pete, emailed Gary V. every day for six months straight.

Set your targets. Study their work, read their books, and learn how they think.

TAKE INITIATIVE

Your productivity is deeply rooted in your self-awareness. Expanding your productivity by becoming more self-aware relies on your imagination and your conscience. Through imagination, we envision what our potential can produce. And through our conscience, we develop beliefs that drive our skills and build our talents, which is why self-awareness adjusts behavior.

This is what empowers us to write our own scripts and why it is important to live out of our imaginations and not our pasts.

Theoretical physicist Albert Einstein's most famous quote is, "Imagination is more important than knowledge."

So, be mindful of the fact that ambitious, hard work brings about the sweetest rewards. It is the ongoing process of keeping your actions aligned with your principles, values, and vision. Success, after all, is having complete control of oneself.

Much like you can be your own worst enemy, you can also be your own best friend. Be especially mindful of how you talk to yourself, for example, and the thoughts and conversations you have in your head, as these have the greatest impact on the things you manifest. This is also the one thing that you are always in complete control of.

For example, don't ever say the word "never." And don't ever say the word "can't." Challenge yourself and consider these words the most harmful, destructive, and limiting words in the English language. Two words, so simple. But they stop your brain from trying to find answers. Making the conscious effort to no longer use these words forces you to find positive ways to say what you mean.

I've had tremendous success by simply replacing the word "can't" with phrases like, "I haven't found a way to do that." Or "I want to figure out the best way." Hearing the word "can't" puts your mind to sleep. It simply gives up. Saying "I don't know how yet" leaves open the possibility of the means being out there. Accepting the challenge, your subconscious goes to work.

One of your biggest impacts will be with those whom you have the most in common and spend the most amount of time with. When preparing to add value, learn your audiences. It could be your team, your staff, your board of directors, a parent teacher association, or the chamber of commerce. Understand their communication styles and establish for yourself how to best communicate your message.

The idea is to add value by eliciting positive emotions and moving them toward your view of your message. Keep in mind that for your message to resound, it must first be accepted on an emotional level. The greatest message can be lost through poor delivery, just as much as on a closed mind. If you know your audience, all it takes is tact. Know your message and speak with intentional delivery; your message along with all its frequency and vibrations will come straight from the heart.

THE VIBE

Throughout the years, I've had the opportunity to implement policy in some of the most cutting-edge sales floors in the most competitive markets. What would always set my teams apart and give us the most competitive advantage was our ability to maintain control of the vibe. The vibe is the energy or the feel of the room. Whether it is a boardroom, the sales floor, or someone's front door, nothing is more important for maintaining focus than the vibe.

It all starts by everyone having the right mindset, followed by the right systems of protocol. To stay sharp, make it a practice to always remove the weakest links. For example, anyone having a negative outlook or who is having a bad day or who simply doesn't have a positive answer to the question, "How do I need to be thinking right now and why?" will have to leave before their energy has a chance to impact the overall vibe. Establishing a system of protocols ahead of time will prevent panic, confusion, and downtime. The key to this is knowing one another's jobs and taking initiative. This sense of security creates the vibe. The ultimate goal is to not skip a beat and instead create momentum with deliberate focus.

TAKEAWAYS

I want to leave you with some important ideas to help guide you on your journey. Write these down, post them, read them, and say them out loud every day to help you focus on maintaining your hard work and your passion to reach your goals.

- Emotions are habits. Limits are liars. And fears are thieves.
- To be successful, you must quickly put your thoughts into action.
- Focus on the positive, and your thinking will move you in a positive direction.
- Don't ever give up. Because you don't know if the next try is going to be the one that works. So, gather good intelligence, choose wisely, and read.
- Want wealth? Get awareness.
- Surround yourself with good thinkers. Avoid time wasters. Instead, spend time with and figure out how your mentors think.
- Write your goals down.
- Live on less than you make and invest the difference. Be decisive when it comes to this. In life, you either make a decision, or one will be made for you.
- Decide. Commit. Act. Succeed. And repeat.
- Be relentless. Demand more of yourself than anyone else could ever demand of you.

Rafael credits his success to his early mentors. Constantly reminded of how incredibly grateful he is for their guidance, Rafael strives to repay their generosity by now mentoring and assisting new and upcoming entrepreneurs himself. Guided by the principals he learned that it is the responsibility of success to reach back and give a hand to those who are coming up.

Now hosting frequent speaking events nationwide to inspire and teach others, Rafael and his wife Amanda travel together while running a growing and successful international sourcing and import business.

Inspirational credits to my brother, Jose, for being my very first business partner; to my son, Mario, who has been my most inspiring business partner; and to his brothers and sisters, whom he'll pass down to. And, most importantly, to the generations of leaders who, like their mentors, will only achieve what their elders reflect to them. May the passages in this book reinforce your search for that three-strand cord that will lead you beyond your most desired and deserved measures.

I commend you.

EVERYONE HAS POTENTIAL, FEW PUT IN THE WORK

JAY ACEVES

Some people look at my life right now and think I have it easy because of what I show them. I have my own apartment, I owned two different BMWs during the past couple of years, and now I'm living in Chicago, traveling back and forth to Los Angeles and Miami. Yeah, I could see where people think my life is amazing. I'm not saying that my life is not amazing, but for a long time I would only show the good and not really be straight up about all the different struggles. I would keep calm and quiet about them and just show all the good things in life. That is, until recently. Why?

People relate to honesty, being humble and passionate, rather than being perfect all the time. You have to look beyond the surface and really understand behind the scenes of what happens and what people are going through. In reality, it hasn't always been easy for me, and there were, and still are, struggles in my life. Whether it is financial, relationship, or business, life is not easy for anyone, and there are always struggles. The questions are, "How are you going to react? How will you turn your struggles or obstacles into success?"

There are going to be roadblocks, there are going to be friendships lost, broken hearts, hard lessons, struggles, successes, and triumphs in your journey. Anything is possible, as long as you do not quit. Rest, but do not quit.

This chapter will be about my journey and my lessons and what I have been through in my life so far, which has led me to become a leader in the community, a business owner, a role model, and a mentor. I have built an empire and legacy for my family and future family. Fall

in love with the process and keep your eyes on the prize.

OBSTACLES OF BEING LATINO

Being Hispanic growing up in an all-white neighborhood, there were different areas where I wasn't fully accepted. It didn't matter how good I was playing baseball, basketball, and soccer. I had a lot of different teammates in high school, yet I never really had a teammate that was my best friend. That was one of the reasons that caused me to do extra work in practice and put in extra time to get better.

When some of these guys were out partying on the weekends or days after a game, I was working on getting better at baseball or working to make money, whether it was at a summer camp, coaching or busing tables, or as a pool attendant at Loews Santa Monica Beach Hotel. Looking back, I do want to give a special thanks to my parents, because they were the ones who installed these values of working hard and being smart about managing my time.

During those years of working, while everyone else was out enjoying the beach and having fun, I was not happy about it and did not agree with my parents at the time. But looking at it now, these are the same things that set me up for success and allowed me to be where I am now. So, thank you, Mom and Dad, for instilling these valuable traits in my life.

WORK ETHIC

I remember when I started working and making a good amount of money. My dad started making me pay my own bills and pay rent for living at home. I always got mad each month when I had to pay $400 to live at home. I never understood why he was making me do that, and I would always hear it from my friends too. Little did I know that my parents were teaching me how to be responsible with my money, because I was making a great amount of money that allowed me access to go do whatever I wanted, buy whatever I wanted (shoes, clothes, watches), and even go out drinking.

Guess what happened to that rent money. When I graduated from college, after the ceremony my parents gave me an envelope, which I thought was a congratulations card. I opened it up and it was a check for $21,000. I was shocked, to say the least, and grateful that they loved me that much to hold that money and save it, so I would be able to have a cushion and not live paycheck to paycheck in life.

This taught me to be smart with my money and not go crazy spending, just because I had it. So many people nowadays live paycheck to paycheck, because they spend money they don't actually have; they are spending their money going toward their bills, and when the end of the month comes, it is a scramble to pay everything or they get behind. A good motto to live by is that you can't afford something unless you can buy it twice (according to American rapper and businessman JAY-Z).

As I still continued to work at the hotel as a bartender, I eventually moved my way up with hard work. I was working long hours, five to six days a week, but again I was making great money. After I graduated from college with my criminal justice degree, I started applying to different police departments to kickstart my journey and become a SWAT officer or a detective. I chose that route, because I've always wanted to help people and show them that there are different ways that things can be done, as long as they have an open mind.

The more I talked to different officers with extended years on the job, the less I wanted to become one. I respect them highly for the job that they do, but the stories they shared, what they saw, and how they almost lost their families made me second-guess everything. So, I continued to work at the hotel, bartending and living a comfortable life, going out all the time and known by all the bouncers at the bars and clubs, the "good life," right? Wrong! I was spending a lot of money and hanging out with people who only wanted to be around me because I had money. The minute I stopped wanting to spend money and go out so much, they were nowhere to be found.

ONE DAY CHANGES THE COURSE OF MY LIFE

One night out changed it all for me. I went to a local bar in Manhattan Beach; I'd been there multiple times before. A few of my friends were performing live. We had a table near the stage and were having a good time. I was in and out, not feeling so good, drunk out of my mind. The bouncers forced me to leave. I got home, somehow, and passed out in the garage of my parents' house. Early in the morning, my parents woke up and went to do laundry. I was lying there unresponsive. To this day, I don't know what happened, because I could handle my liquor more than I actually drank that night. But what changed my lifestyle for me was what my mom said to me later that day.

Of course, my parents were both mad, but they were more concerned and scared about me, because they said they tried waking me up for a long period of time, and I was not moving. They were afraid that I was dead. I thought about what she said—to imagine me dying and having my parents and sisters bury me felt like a stake went through my heart.

That night I decided to never get that drunk ever again, and I had to do something about my health and my life. I wanted to live up to my potential and not waste my talents anymore trying to please people. That was an eye-opening event to have to look at myself and ask, "What are you doing with your life?" And I couldn't see anything in my future.

OPEN TO OPPORTUNITIES

It's funny what opportunities arrive when you make the decision to change. I was looking for a way to help thousands of people, but not become a police officer. That is exactly what I am doing now, helping people live fit, inspiring them to take action in their own lives, and building a network of coaches who support hundreds and thousands of clients. My business creates healthy, active, lifestyle communities worldwide and is leading into a multimillion-dollar business fueled by people getting fit and unleashing their inner athlete.

It didn't start that way, as there was a lot I had to go through before this was even on my radar to do as a business and a career. I needed to find myself again and become fit, athletic, happy, and confident. So, I started working out extra to get my healthy, active lifestyle back as an athlete. I had to get my health back, because working as a bartender and partying at night caused me to gain a bunch of weight. I was all the way up to 281 pounds, my heaviest, and if I didn't change, I knew my life was headed to become another statistic of a Hispanic man with diabetes and other health issues.

I knew how to work out. I have done it all my life, playing various sports, so I put myself in the gym, working out six to seven days a week after an 8 to 10-hour shift at work. I was able to lose about 25 pounds in four months, but I gained it back in one month after losing focus. It was a constant yo-yo for me to lose 20 pounds, gain 30 pounds, back-and-forth, back-and-forth, and finally I decided to take my friend up on an offer that I had put off for eight months straight.

I started a customized program for me of what to eat and how to fuel before, during, and after workouts. I partnered with Herbalife nutrition. I had tried plenty of other supplements and products and worked out before and nothing helped, so my mindset was kind of skeptical about this, but I decided to make it happen because Jake lost 75 pounds following the plan, and I knew him.

When I do anything, I usually like to go all in, but for some reason I still was 50-50 on this. But within two weeks of following the plan and program that he created for me, I lost 12 pounds. This is when I started to take this on 100 percent, and in six months I lost 40 pounds, which was my goal.

In January, I joined a challenge—there were more than 340 participants at Redondo Sports Nutrition. I was blown away by how many people were getting their body fat test done to register and the great feeling I got being around all these people. That's when I sat down with Jake's mentor and coach, Meera (before she became my best friend and novia), and went over my goals for the challenge. She invited me to attend some of the weekly workouts.

I started attending the workouts, and in four-and-a-half months, I lost another 46 pounds, totaling 87 pounds weight lost and dropping 26 percent body fat—the best shape of my life. I found myself feeling at the top of my game, like an athlete again, and life started to become happier. I can honestly say that being around the community of people, all pushing toward their own goals but doing it together, helped me not plateau at 40 pounds but helped me push myself in additional workouts. This was one step more, which allowed me not to quit and accomplish this amazing transformation in the process.

I share that with you, because it's not just about eating right; it's not just about working out right; but it's about that plus attitude of being around people who are likeminded. Every journey is going to have roadblocks—that's a given, but if you're alone, it's a lot easier to quit on yourself. On the other hand, when you have people holding you, if you miss a day, they text and ask you what's going on? Are you OK? Can I help you with anything? That is the key. Nothing in this life is worth it, if you do not have people to share it with. You need your squad to have your back and cheer you on in the times of struggle.

MINDSET IS KEY

It is the same thing in business today. I hang out with individuals who have things that I want, and who I would trade places with. We are building a fitness and nutrition empire and to get that, you have to build a team that is "ride or die" with you, who will not allow your excuses to get in the way of the bigger picture. Be around people who will take a stand for you, who will force you to level up. You cannot build an empire based on feelings and do things when they are convenient to you. You need to finish the task at hand as soon as possible, but be effective. You have to be careful who you spend your time with, because they will influence outcomes in your life. I know that you see quotes and sayings on social media, but they are 100 percent true that if you hang out with five broken people, you are bound to be the next one. However, on the opposite end, if you hang out with five successful people, you are bound to be successful, if you continue to do the work.

Have you ever noticed how the negative person is always the person attracting more negative stuff? I watch people on social media. The negative person just posted how so much negative stuff happens to them. They talk about how negative the week is going. How everyone around them at work is so negative. How they just got a flat tire. How they just got a ticket. How they just got stuck having to pay a bill that they shouldn't have to pay. I'm not trying to call any one person out. And if you're the person who I'm talking about, I'm sorry if you take it personal. Negativity is a choice. What you put out, comes back to you. There's a reason why the happy person is always happy, doing happy things with a bunch of other happy people.

This is probably one of the toughest areas to work on, because this is personal development. It is personal to you and what you are going through at that moment of your life. It could be about financial situations, relationships, positive outlooks, gaining confidence, business networking, but the X factor is YOU!

Just like success, **you** have to put in the time and the work to make it happen; it just won't happen out of sheer luck. Some of my mentors in personal development (through books or audio files) are Jim Rohn, Eric Thomas, Mark Hughes, Gary Vaynerchuk, Tony Robbins, and Napoleon Hill. These mentors have all helped me develop into the successful leader I am today. In addition, I had the help of my parents and their values they shared with me. This is a perfect time to start working on yourself daily, build your routine to help yourself function at your highest level, and accomplish the most possible.

WILLING TO DO TO SUCCEED

The decision to move to Chicago was not easy. Yes, I chose to expand here, and no one forced me to. To be successful, you have to organize your priorities. I understood what this move would allow me to access, to accomplish the goals that I want to be able to provide for my family, my sisters, and my future family. This was a big move for me, because family is such a big piece of my life, and I have always had them right by my side, from meeting every Thursday at my grandma's house with all my cousins, to not having that for three or six months at a time. That's tough.

In the long run, it will be worth it, as long as I do the work. I share that with you, because sometimes we get caught up in what life throws at us or we get caught up in enjoying life too much and not focusing on the real reason we're here. So many times, I have been caught up in going out when I have not finished my DMO and hit my number. I am not saying not to go have fun, but go have fun **after** you finish what your goal was for the day.

What is a DMO? It's your daily method of operation. Whatever business you are in, you have to find your flow of what will work for you and how it will help you get closer to your goals. Whether it's presenting your product to a certain number of people, going to 20 business meetings for potential clients to get one, the key is finding your flow. If you need to travel or move to a different city to accomplish your goals, I would recommend you look at that as opportunity for growth and see what you can do to help make it happen.

STRUGGLES

Like I said earlier, there are struggles in life and this year has been full of them for me, yet there are so many opportunities rising and doors opening. Why? Because I have kept going instead of looking at myself as a victim to my circumstances. Nowadays, people give up the minute it gets hard, because they want the instant gratification, but life does not work that way. Imagine if you knew you were going to get five flat tires this year, would you be as upset at each flat tire? No, because you knew you were almost there. It is key to understand that in life and business when you hustle, your life is going to look like a roller coaster.

It has also been tough this past year for me, because things have not gone according to plan with business, finances, and traveling. We mapped out our business and what we projected, and it has not been quite there. That is the beauty of being an entrepreneur—you have your ups and downs, but you're always open to new opportunities and new ideas and always looking for ways to accomplish those goals.

For example, living in Chicago, I have not been on top of my spending habits as much as I should, because I wanted to enjoy the city and the food, so I would order food all the time, go on adventures, and I had to dip into my savings account more than I wished. Some of you might be saying, "At least you have a savings account." You will read about that later. One of my goals is not to live paycheck to paycheck and not worry about bills. If I did not catch myself, I would soon be in that situation.

One thing that I came to realize really quickly was that Chicago is a different beast than Los Angeles—people act differently, people live differently, people work differently, and that's what takes time to understand and to build relationships so we can empower them to take charge of their lives and not sacrifice their security for happiness, so they can have both. The beauty of moving to a city that is foreign to me is that I was forced to grow as an individual through the process and get better at building relationships. Through that, I have made some amazing friendships in Chicago.

I have been able to network with other talented and hard-working individuals across the city and help them build their empires. This only happened because I was open to change and be coachable to becoming better. Being coachable does not mean you have to agree on everything your mentor or mentors are teaching you. It means that you must be open to new ideas and open to applying them. If you are not coachable, you will only get so far in life until you keep running into the same roadblocks.

I do suggest that you evaluate your life right now, and ask yourself, "Am I doing what I love every single day? If not, how can I do more of what I love and turn that passion into a business so I never have to 'work' another day in my life?" It can be whatever your passion is, but remember you will hit roadblocks, so find your squad of people who will support you, but also keep it real. Have that work ethic to make it happen, no matter how long it takes, and be sure to work on yourself daily.

Look around—it's time to wake up and not be a zombie like everyone else. Stand up for who you really are.

Thank you for reading my chapter. If you have any questions, feel free to email me at aacevesj89@gmail.com. If you want help with your health and fitness goals or to collaborate on business, build with us globally, email and check out mjfitsquad.com.

I want to thank everyone putting *The Hustle Code* together and the authors for sharing their success tips on life in their areas of expertise. Take notes and always be a student of life.

Jay Aceves is an ex athlete who went from winning championships to sitting on the couch playing video games, taking naps and being lazy.

After college, he found himself over weight & tired, partying multiple days a week to fit in & "live life to the fullest" but something needed to change. He needed to tap into his inner athlete, that championship mentality, things changed dramatically, he has been able to lose 87lbs and keep it off for over 2 years and found that inner athlete and passion about life.

He is passionate about helping people find their inner athlete and playing the game of life, tap into their reserve tank and bring their greatness out!

FROM JUVENILE OFFENDER TO FAMILY DEFENDER

BERNIE GERMANI

CHILDHOOD

I grew up in Brooklyn, New York, with a dad, who was second-generation Italian, and a mom, who was from Puerto Rico. I had what I thought was a good childhood. My neighborhood was mainly Italians, Dominicans, and Puerto Ricans, all mixed together. For the most part, we all got along well, as there were many kids my age. This made it interesting, as our block was also known as el barrio para estar fuera de si no viven en el bloque (the neighborhood to stay out of, if you did not live on the block). The reason was because if others came to our block, they were chased away, beaten, or robbed.

Everyone had older brothers, but me, so we were always protected by them. I was known as half-breed, because I was the only kid on the block who was not one specific nationality, but I could speak to everyone in Spanish and Italian. I was also mature for my age, hung out with the older kids, and learned how to fight at an early age. I got to represent our block in fighting other neighborhoods. Sometimes I would lose, but many times I would win, and sometimes I was rewarded with money from the older kids.

My dad didn't want me to fight anymore; he said I could actually start working for him. So, long story short, I became a kid who ran numbers for local bookies, basically running around town picking up numbers, then bringing to my dad, which he in turn paid me for each bookie's number. This is when I learned that I would never want to work for someone else—I'll do this forever and move up later with different jobs.

Well, needless to say that didn't last too long and, at 10 years old, I had my first encounter with law enforcement. I never told the real truth, so I mentioned to the police that some guy paid me money to pick up envelopes and take them to different places around town, but I was to never know what was inside. The police called my dad, and he had to come pick me up from the police station. At the station, he pretended to be mad, but in the car, he told me how proud he was of me for not saying anything to the police, and I would be rewarded when we got home, which I was. My mom was furious and said we were moving to California, which we did shortly afterwards, because she didn't want me to be a street thug.

We were in California for about a year. Apparently, my mom wanted nothing to do with my dad's business dealings anymore, and she decided to leave my dad, me, my sister, and me. To this day, I have never seen my mom nor would I even know what she looks like, if she walked in front of me today. After that time, I had little contact with her family which ultimately, all communication stopped, and we lost all contact with every member of my mom's family.

I hated California because my family was ripped apart, I had no friends, and I felt alone. My dad was trying to raise two children on his own, as best as he could, but it was difficult for him, my sister, and me. We no longer spoke Spanish or Italian, because there was no one to talk to in our language, so English was all we could speak. Legit jobs were difficult for my dad to adjust to, and so he went through many jobs. A few years later, my dad remarried my stepmom (I call her mom, though, as if she were my biologically mom) however, that was trying on us, as she had a son.,We had to try to get along with him, but it was difficult.

My dad worked so hard at so many jobs. He was miserable because he no longer could live his way of making money. He was working for many different companies, with many different jobs. He had started a few businesses;they all failed. However, I saw something in my dad that I had never seen before, which was no matter how many times he failed, he kept getting back up.

I watched my dad struggle to make an honest way of living, which bothered me, because we appeared to be flourishing in New York, and yet my dad was working all the time, and we did not seem to have the money we had previously. I started cutting neighbors' lawns, and I had a few paper routes, which I despised, but these jobs taught me a few things about myself: that I could always make money, and I learned sales, which allowed me to explain to my neighbors why it was to their best benefit to have me cut their lawn, as it would free up more of their time to be with the family on Saturday instead of working outside.

Because everyone trusted me, I plotted the most perfect plan to make a lot more money by breaking into my neighbors' houses and then pawning jewelry or taking cash to help my dad, which I did, until I finally got caught. I was 13, so I was released to my parents without a record. I was a troubled teenager, mainly because our family didn't have money. I had a stepbrother, a stepmother I still really didn't like, and I watched my dad go down the straight and narrow path, which really bothered me. I thought I'd show him what I could accomplish.

For the next five years, I was in and out of juvenile hall. I did everything from stealing cars, to selling drugs, to credit card fraud. I would steal anything I possibly could get away with, and I had lots of money. It was getting so bad that my parents could not even control me anymore; my dad said I would be in jail for the rest of my life, or I would be dead. There was one more event that took place, as I was embezzling lots of money from a business that got me kicked out of my house. I was probably going to jail for a long time. Little did I know my life was going to be a living hell for the next three years; however, it would also change my life forever for the better.

MILITARY TIME

I didn't know that my dad had become friends with a US Marine across the street. My dad told this guy all about me—how much trouble I had been in and all the recent trouble that would probably end up with me in jail. Little did I know that the Marines, my dad, and the courts struck a deal together, and that once I turned 18, I would be off to the Marines for the next four years. The day I turned 18, the people where I was staying had my bags packed, and I thought they were kicking me out, but that was not the case.

Two Marines came to the door to get me. One was the neighbor across the street from my parent's house. I tried to run out the back door, and I managed to escape briefly, as I kept jumping block wall after wall, until I came to an alley. There were two more Marines waiting for me. I tried to fight them, but it didn't work out so well; however, I was intrigued how quickly they were able to take me down. I wanted to learn how they took me down so quickly, but I still did not want to go into the Marine Corps.

My first year in the Marines was the most miserable. I hated every aspect of the Marines, and every way I tried to get out, they had a counterattack against me. I finally said, for my own sanity, it was probably time to not be a rebel and become the best man I could be. The Gulf War/ Operation Desert Storm took place in August 1990, with the invasion of Kuwait, through February 1991. During that time, I got many wakeup calls that my life had a bigger purpose, and that I was meant for greatness.

The whole next year I got to patrol the Embassies in Colombia and Venezuela. That was the most enjoyable time of my Marine service. I got to know who I was as a man, knew my four years was coming to an end, but also realized I was no longer a lone ranger. I needed to have a good team around me. The military truly molded me into the man I am today, and I knew that I would never give up on life or my dreams and goals.

After I was honorably discharged, I knew I had to make things right with my family, which I did. I thanked my dad for saving my life, even though I hated him and wanted nothing to do with him when I was 18, and I had no contact with him the entire four years I was gone. My dad truly became a man I admired, respected, and loved deeply.

STARTING MY CAREER

A year after the military, I decided to go to college, and chose to El Camino College in Torrance, California. Then I transferred to California State University, Dominguez Hills, graduating with a bachelor's degree in business administration, as I knew I wanted to own my business someday. During school, I wanted to make money the legal way and always found an attraction to network marketing, and real estate, so I joined many different networking companies, but I was really starting to love real estate.

I would go to real estate events, meet top Realtors, and ask if they would teach me the business. A few said yes, but nothing really materialized, as I needed to get a job because I was getting married in 1996. I went to work for Sparkletts water for a short time; however, it changed my life, because it led me to doing social work. I ended up going back to school for my masters in social work, so I could become a social worker for the county of Los Angeles in historic South Central Los Angeles. I loved the work; however, there was always a lot of red tape, which frustrated me and hindered my job. I had some of the most difficult cases in all South Central.

The year was 2000, and I had bumped into one of my old Sparkletts customers who was driving a brand-new Porsche, which I was so in awe of, as that was my dream car. I started to ask questions and found out he was doing loans, I discovered how easy the money was. I kept asking him if it was legal, and he mentioned repeatedly how much money could be made by doing loans for mortgages. That would allow me to live the lifestyle I so desperately wanted. On my off days, I would ask this guy to teach me the loan business, as I went to work part-time for him while still working for the county. In 2003, I finally left the county to do loans full-time, and wow, what a ride it was.

In January 2004, my mentor passed away unexpectedly, which caused a lot of anxiety, and I literally had no income coming in. I had managed to save money from the volume of loans to sustain me for awhile. The owner's wife, shortly after his passing, knew I couldn't sustain his office or business, and she decided to shut the company down. The day I packed all my stuff and was walking out the door, Francesca told me, "Bernie, you have a great knack for numbers and the mortgage business. You should eventually open your own company."

I told her that was the goal, and that I would call her, once I opened my doors. That was a profound statement, as I knew that's exactly what I had strived for, but wasn't quite ready for that opportunity. I found another mortgage originator position fairly quickly in Orange County, the haven for subprime mortgages.

In June 2004, I told the current owner that I was not happy, as I was one of his top originators, and my income didn't reflect that. I asked him for 1.5 points on all deals I originated. He had the biggest laugh and told me to get back to hustling the phones. I said, "Sir, no disrespect to you, but I'm worth more than what you're paying me, and I will not go back to the phones until I get my points to 1.5."

He looked at me and said, "Are you deaf and stupid?"

I said, "I'm sorry. What did you just say?"

So he repeated himself. I wanted to harm this guy, but I had learned some great coping skills in the military and in my work at the county, so I walked over to him and whispered, "If you ever talk to me like that again, I will rip your eyes from your face." Then I told him I was just kidding, sort of, and that I quit. I said, "As a matter of fact, I promise you I will open a mortgage company right down the street from here, and I will make it my life mission to close your doors, because of the way you treat people."

In July 2004, I opened my net branch mortgage company, literally three blocks from the previous mortgage company. I worked around the clock, only taking Sunday off. During the next two years, I had six mortgage originators working with me and three processors. We did 119 million dollars in volume, all in subprime loans. I became an arrogant person, and if you were not part of my team, I wanted nothing to do with you, nor would I want to even meet you.

I also developed heart issues for the first time in my life. My doctor said if I didn't slow down I would be dead in six months. I took a vacation for the first time in years, tried reconnecting with my wife and my son, which we did for a short period of time, then right back to the grind.

My passion for putting my former mortgage company out of business consumed my being, and it fueled my passion to close it down. I would stop at nothing. I started farming his clients. All the places he wanted to do business, I was there first. I was not at peace, had a lot of turmoil in my life, and became unpleasant to be around, even though the money was ridiculous. I did not have balance in my life, and my health was quickly deteriorating. I was not happy.

In September 2006, I decided I needed help, so I started with counseling and finding a successful mentor in the mortgage business. I started meeting with my mentor once a week to lay out my business, and she would help strategize, reorganize, and structure my calendar. I eventually got an assistant, which made my life so much easier.

In December 2006, my mentor told me, "Bernie, this is the last time we will be meeting. You don't need me anymore, as your life is back on track, your health is doing better, and I don't feel right taking your money anymore." On my way out the door, she said, "Bernie, I'm going to leave you with some advice. Please take it very seriously."

I told her that of course I would. She said, "Promise me you will stop your spending, stop buying properties, and start to put all your money away and prepare yourself with your family, as we are going to have one of the worst market crashes of all times, and you will lose everything."

I looked at her with a blank stare, laughed slightly, and said, "What you are talking about?"

I sat back down and for the next hour she started to explain why the real estate market was going to crash. We finished our conversation. I gave her a hug, thanked her for her time, and told her that we would catch up later. I walked to my car, thinking, *This lady is off her rocker, she must be out of her mind.* There wasn't going to be any crash.

The first quarter of 2007 was crazy busy, and we couldn't work fast enough to keep up with the volume of loans. I hired one more originator and processor. I called my previous mentor and told her what was going on. She reminded me to trust her and told me that the crash would happen that year. She told me to not buy anymore properties and to start putting all my money away. (I told her I didn't take her advice, but would get around to it.)

The second quarter of 2007 was the worst quarter I had during my entire stint in the business, but I started to notice some interesting things going on. I noticed a lot more FBI agents around Orange County. I then started to hear of companies starting to close their doors, and then I got a phone call from a previous friend who told me that the former company I worked for was being shut down for fraud, Many people were arrested there. I called my mentor and told her what was going on. She told me that she had warned me and that it was about to get even uglier. I still thought, *Why is she still talking about this doom and gloom? She is clearly misinformed.*

The third quarter of 2007 was worse than the second quarter. I didn't really panic, but knew I needed to make some moves, so I flipped my first property in Hawthorne for some extra money. I didn't know a thing about it, but I trusted the person who I partnered with. I also started to refinance a few of my rental properties to pull cash out, keep up payroll, and manage the business expenses.

The fourth quarter of 2007 rolled around, but I was feeling optimistic. Early on in the quarter, I noticed more companies going out of business; banks were being shut down; and my lender, who I gave about 90 percent of my business to, came in and said, "Something is going on. I think we are closing our doors." I told him that was impossible, as his company was the largest subprime company in the market place.

From October to December of 2007, I saw share pandemonium, and people lose everything.

In March 2008, I closed my doors. When I got home, I remember curling up on the kitchen floor and crying, because I didn't know what to do anymore and felt my life was over. The next six months I was depressed. I was a pathetic man and did nothing but cry all day. That took a toll on my wife, and she said if I didn't get my act together, she was leaving. I didn't even care, but knew I couldn't stay like that.

I got back into flipping homes, but the money I made was to pay back people and try to make things right with them, but it wasn't happening fast enough. My story goes like many others—I lost everything, had to file for bankruptcy, and, on top of that, my money manager swindled me out of $300K, which later made headlines all throughout Orange County, because there were many others he did that to.

I decided I wasn't going to let that define me, as I watched my dad early on go through failures, and knew I could bounce back. I started to find the real Bernie, get out of my depression and funk to be the best me. I lost weight and got into the best shape of my life. I just knew I could make the comeback; I was determined, until 2010 rolled around.

2010—THE YEAR I ALMOST GAVE UP ON LIFE

My wife and I tried counseling. It didn't work out, and we were set for divorce. Ten days before our first court appearance, the rock of my life, my dad, passed away from a massive heart attack. I had a huge, gaping hole left trying to deal with the divorce and my son.

Ten days after my court appearance, my cousin from New York was visiting me in California, and he happened to be in the wrong place at the wrong time. Someone took his life, which left me with anger, and I wanted to avenge his life. I searched high and low for the two cowards who killed him, but I never found them. I decided I would let the police do their job. To this day, the killers have not been caught.

I had a lot of rage and became reckless. I wanted to kill my ex-wife, but knew if I did that, I would go to jail. Then my son would have neither parent. I decided I would kill myself. That night, I pulled the trigger, but my gun jammed, which it had never done before, so the gun never fired. I dropped the gun and started praying to God, "Lord, please help me... If you're there, listen to my prayers. I need you now."

I decided to check myself into the VA Hospital to get some help. I was there for 10 days, got myself back together, and started working to find Bernie again. I finally got myself back on track with even greater vigor than when I started in the mortgage business. I knew that God's plan for my life must be amazing. I wanted to go back into social services, even though I started flipping properties again. I needed steady income to get me back on track.

I worked for a nonprofit in South Central Los Angeles, working with troubled youth again. I stayed for three years, while I kept flipping properties; however, due to circumstances out of my control, the nonprofit terminated my contract. Instead of being bitter about it, I used that for motivation to go full force into my passion of real estate and flipping properties. I don't want to say everything is perfect, because it's not. I still have struggles; I still have regrets in not listening to my mentor about everything she shared with me. I'm still rebuilding, but I keep moving forward daily. Do times get tough? Yes, but I know now that I believe I have hit the bottom, and now I can only bounce back up with my loving God next to my side.

CONCLUSION

I want to thank you for reading my chapter. Even though I don't know you personally, I know you were meant for greatness, but you have to want it badly enough to go get it. Life can be harsh at times, and it will continue to be harsh. But how do we respond when life does throw us those curveballs? We keep pushing regardless, because the fact that we aren't where we should be, should be enough motivation.

I want to thank my dad for all his life lessons that I never knew were lessons until I got older and had my own son. I understand what you did for me and Gina. I want to thank a coauthor of this book, Edgar Hurtado, for being a true man of your word and always seeing the bigger picture.

I also want to thank Ryan Garland from Paradyme Funding, as your wisdom is beyond your young years. You continue to believe in me, even at times when I don't believe in myself, and you are a great role model to have in my life.

My son, Michael, who just graduated from high school, I'm so proud of you for working your butt off to graduate with your class of 2017. I love you so much. My mom, two sisters, and my brother—I love you guys so much, and thank you for being in my life.

PROMOTING POSITIVE COMMUNITY & ECONOMIC GROWTH IN OUR NEIGHBORHOODS.

Bernie Germani, Chairman of the Board of BM Trust, has been deeply involved in California real estate as a master planner, master builder, and long-term investor for 17 years.

Raised in Hawthorne, California from a young age, Bernie served in The Marines earned his E4 Corporal ranking. Bernie obtained a degree in business administration from Cal State Dominguez, and then a Masters Degree in Social Work from the University of Southern California.

Bernie has envisioned a true education for those desiring more one on one and mentoring. Taking an industry riddled by promises of overnight success, Bernie wanted to stand out by simply sharing the truth. Bernie provides those who want real estate investing education that derives from his personal investing experience and strategies he learns from other successful real estate investors around the country.

Bernie owns a company called BM Trust and BMT Consulting Group that manages his real estate holdings and flips. Bernie has done 52 personal flips in his lifetime with more on the horizon. This not only allows him to build wealth and legacy, but keeps him active on the ever changing real estate market so he can share what he learns with his students.

CHARITY WORK

Bernie sits on a board for a domestic violence nonprofit, and spends a lot of time consulting, planning how to improve Los Angeles County's shelters. Bernie also works with Titus Single Parents

Ministry, helping single parents obtain resources for their families. Bernie volunteers his time as well doing child monitoring through Department of Children and Family Services to reunite children with their parents. Bernie also facilitates Divorce Care at his local church twice a year.

ADAPTING TO ADVERSITY

EDUARDO VELEZ

I had a rude awakening at the age of eight. My life changed from having a normal home environment in one of the most immense cities in the world (Mexico City) to nearly becoming a homeless family. In the fall of 1982, my parents spoke with me and told me that we were leaving Mexico for good, and we would permanently live in California. By that time, I had experienced a couple of trips to the United States and had visited Disneyland as a young child and thought, *Wow, this is amazing!* All I could think about was Mickey Mouse, American candy, beautiful weather, and lots of fun.

Of course, I had no idea there was a big difference between visiting as tourists and basically starting a new life. By this time, I had two older brothers living in Roseville, Northern California, and one sister in Los Angeles, California. They had already begun their journey living in the United States. My parents decided to sell everything in Mexico and collected enough money to live comfortably for a few months prior to finding jobs in California.

We arrived at my oldest brother's house in Roseville. He lived with his wife and two children. For us, it was my parents, and my 18-year-old sister, who was closest to me in age. She and I were single at that time.

NEW LIVING ENVIRONMENT

We began our new life in Northern California in the winter of 1982. I went from living in a five-bedroom home in Mexico City to sleeping on a small mattress shared with my sister. The house was old with no type of insulation; it was definitely the worst and coldest winter of my entire life.

By this time school signups were underway, and I had to continue my third-grade elementary school year. This was also a moment in my life where I felt completely out of place. I was introduced to a school which mostly Anglo with a smaller percentage of African Americans, Hispanics, and Asians.

Luckily, there were two professors who spoke Spanish in the school, and there was a program available for students learning English as a second language. During my previous academic years in Mexico, I was considered a B+ grade student, and, to my eyes, my whole school curriculum had turned on me a full 360 degrees.

The hardest part was dealing with the language barrier. When I started school, it was obvious that my appearance with clothing was different from the rest of the kids. I rapidly became a timid kid, due to these circumstances. This led to many days of bullying from a good number of schoolmates who enjoyed picking on the new weird-looking kid.

Not only was I living in a completely different world, but I had also lost the support academically from my mother. She was not able to assist with homework or any school assignment, because she did not speak English. Adjustments became part of the norm, and I began to adapt to the changes, little by little, at school. I had learned to deal with school on my own terms, which consequently affected my grades by becoming a satisfactory C- grade student.

Some of my memories about this stage of my life are played in my mind as extreme, from extremely joyful to extremely sad and depressing. As a child, I was able to learn and meet kids from the neighborhood and learned all the American games and sports. The days were full of playtime and learning.

As time went, by my parents were struggling through the worst time of their life financially. The family funds were scarce; we had practically no money for daily food and everyday necessities. We relied on a local church that assisted the homeless with food such as bread, cheese, eggs, fruits, and other food items.

I clearly remember one late afternoon when I walked a few miles with my parents on our way to pick up this food from the church. In the middle of a storm, we were walking and carrying the heavy bags and were completely soaked from the rain. During this moment, I felt sad, but in a way also joyful, because the family was blessed with food to take home.

Nowadays when I remember this moment, I feel heartache and sorrow for remembering my parents having to deal with such a struggle. Unfortunately, we came to the point where we needed money, and one of the resources was to collect aluminum cans from Dumpsters. I remember climbing into the large trash containers next to apartment buildings or in community parks to collect the cans. By this time, as a child, I completely understood our financial situation and learned not to ask my parents for anything extra, unlike other kids in my school who would want a particular brand of shoes, Atari games, or trips to local recreational places. As a nine-year-old boy, my living experiences made me speed up my maturing process.

The struggles became heavier and more intense, as the poverty was getting extreme. My parents began to disconnect as a married couple and had strong fights and disagreements. By this time, my father had become unemployed and had worked in many different odd jobs that were not of his trade. He became depressed and found himself relying on alcohol to soothe his pain. It was suddenly 1985, when things were the toughest. It was a breaking point, where my family desperately was seeking a change.

My sister had become engaged and was ready to marry. Her wedding was the beginning of the end for our life in Northern California. The separation between my sister and me was devastating—she was a role model for me, she was my partner and protector, as she always looked after me with so much love and care.

A few months after the wedding, my mother had a serious talk with me. She said "We will leave this town, just you and me. We will go live in Los Angeles with your other sister and her family. Your father will no longer be with us." These were the most crushing words I had ever heard in my life, as my tears started to drip down my cheeks. I told my mother that I didn't want to leave my father. My heart was completely torn as we both cried and hugged.

My mother said that we would have a better future together, but the decision was made—we would leave with or without my father. My mother felt my deep sadness and approached my father by letting him know this was his last opportunity to stop drinking for him to maintain his family together. He agreed to make the trip to Los Angeles in the summer of 1986.

SUNNY SOUTHERN CALIFORNIA

My father owned an older, Ford, yellow station wagon, which was the only asset that the family owned at that time. We loaded the car with a few personal items and the three of us decided to make the trip to Los Angeles. The car had the long bench seat in front, able to seat three passengers, where we all sat together for the long drive. I remember my parents being so afraid to make the eight-hour drive at night without speaking English or being able to read any English. And they didn't really understand how to completely read the paper road map.

Both of my parents told me, "Son, you need to stay awake throughout the whole trip, because you will be our guide in reading the road signs on the freeway throughout the night." I remember I was feeling happy due to our family being united and felt proud that my parents were relying on me for guidance. I was overly focused on the road, reading all the signs as we drove, making sure we would not end up on the wrong road.

We finally made it to the big city, and I still remember my parents bragging about me being the one who practically guided the family to Los Angeles. Immediately after arriving, my father searched for employment in his field of expertise in the automotive paint industry and instantly found a job, as his knowledge and experience was second to none. We lived with my sister, Adriana, and her family while my parents were getting back on their feet again.

In the summer of 1986, my father suffered a heart attack during work and was hospitalized for about a month. Fortunately, his employer was understanding and valued him and his work, so was therefore patient to wait for his recovery. Once he was allowed to work part-time during the recovery, my mother asked me to stay by his side while I was on vacation from school, as my father was returning to work.

I was 12 and happy to take care of my father. This was an opportunity for me to learn from my father as I assisted him during work. My father had a completely different strict and strong personality during work. He was so dedicated and disciplined. His way of teaching me was old school—normally he would direct me, as if I was going through boot camp in the military, even using profanity toward me. During this time, I was, for the first time, introduced to real proper hard work, and it was not the same as collecting aluminum cans. This was professional work that had to be done correctly. A company depended on the quality of it.

I was able to learn my father's craft and became good at it. His skill was in automotive paint color matching. After the summer ended, and I was ready to start junior high school, I quickly became a mature young adult. Yes, I was a teenager, but I also began to work every Saturday developing my father's craft and making a little bit of money.

This was something I really enjoyed doing, as I am to this day proud of the skills I honed. In my teenage years, I also was leaving behind my strong Hispanic accent and perfecting my pronunciation of the English language. Life was what I would call normal for a typical Californian teen living in Los Angeles at that time.

SUMMARY OF LIFE ACHIEVEMENTS AND DISAPPOINTMENTS

These are some of my achievements after going through adversity as an immigrant child in the United States.

- I graduated from high school in 1992.
- I then attended a community college, transferring to an engineering career at ITT Tech.
- I graduated with a science and technology engineering degree in 1995.
- I was able to help launch and manage a family paint company that stayed in business for 15 years.
- I worked for a Canadian company, where I represented international companies from different parts of the globe.
- I was able to travel to different countries for sales training in Canada, Germany, Mexico, and England.
- In 2010, I started my own corporation and became an entrepreneur at the age of 36.
- I now also work for a world-class British company in the same field following my father's footsteps, working in the automotive repair industry.
- I am proud to be the only Hispanic in the company with an upper management position, in charge of

sales and development for one of the most important regions of company.

In my personal life, I have been faced with the D word, "divorce." Believe me, I do not regret anything from my past, and I thank my family who has always been there for me in all the ups and downs during my life. By far, my biggest and most precious achievement is when God gave me the opportunity to become the father of a wonderful, healthy boy who is the light of my life. One of my most important goals is to take the challenge that God put in my hands and to raise my child with love and give him my wisdom, earned throughout my life, so his life will be better than my own.

SOME WORDS OF WISDOM

As a Mexican American, I would like to mention, "Do not be afraid to fail." If you do fail, you will learn. Have the courage to try again, and do things better the second time around. We need to remember that being an American is a privilege and that we need to take all the opportunities this country has for us. Learn and ask questions from the many immigrants who have become Americans.

Be a role model to your own children or to children in general. First, make sure they believe in a higher power, no matter what the name of the God might be. Second, transmit deep and sincere love to your child by using powerful and encouraging words that will fill his or her soul with confidence so the child might pass it on to families and friends. Third, teach your children at an early age to be independent. This is important, especially because they need to value hard work, which will lead them to become strong, mature, young adults.

Please always keep in mind that it doesn't matter how difficult your struggle might be at any point of your life; it will be momentary and will pass. Better times will come! Keep your mind focused on the solutions, then take action on them immediately. Then the actions will open the doors for you for better opportunities to reach your ultimate goals.

When making a decision, whether it is a large project or simply just making your bed in the morning, give your best to the project and do it to the best of your ability. Sometimes it is best not to do it, if you do not give it all you have.

Sometimes, we believe we are alone in our difficulties or in any issue we encounter. Remember, we have many resources around us. Seek an opinion from someone who has passed through your situation and has managed to overcome it. Look for help online, use the Internet for self-help for your benefit. Sometimes, we look for the practical solutions and forget the basics, like connecting with ourselves. We need time to take a walk and reset our thoughts. In our communities, we have spiritual events or churches that might be of help. The key is to never feel alone and seek help immediately by looking for the resources.

Last, but not least, be passionate in your life. Try to find feeling in all your endeavors. Connect with anyone you come in contact with and ask sincere questions; sometimes we forget that we are all human and most of us go through the same life issues or situations where we can share with one another.

Even if you take a walk in the park, enjoy it to the fullest—look at the beauty in the trees, see how the sun reflects the water in the pond. Look for something that ignites your life in a positive way and enjoy it by allowing yourself that quality time. Without *passion*, life can become routine. Do not let this happen to you.

AMAZING OPPORTUNITY

I would like to thank all of you for taking the time to read this book and allowing me to tell my story. My purpose and wish is that you might be able to use my past life experiences, and hopefully my story will touch your heart in some way where you might benefit in your personal or professional life. My best wishes to you on your path to success.

SMART HUSTLE

MARCOS OROZCO

I fought many battles in life.. drugs, alcohol, depression and ridicule.. One thing I learned is that Hustle is what keeps me going.. But what is hustle? It means different things to different people. To me, the first time I heard hustle, was on a practice field for a baseball team I was playing second base for. I was about 9 years old, and the coach was telling me to hustle. I'm not sure how I knew exactly what that meant, but to me, it meant to keep pushing forward. Even though I was tired, even though I was out of breath, even though I was sweating, even though my body hurt. I kept going. To me, hustle means you keep pushing forward towards your goal.

To somebody else, hustle actually has a negative meaning. It's doing illegal things, selling illegal products, or doing activities in the street. It's like a thug, an entrepreneur thug.

Everyone has different levels of Hustle. I wanted to use an acronym for the words Hustle Code to describe how I personally hustle..

H stands for Hustle. Hustle to me is working hard even when you don't feel like it.. Waking up early in the morning even if you only slept a couple of hours the night before. It means making that extra sales call. It means not being able to attend happy hour with friends because you have big dreams to fulfill. It means getting back up when life punches you in the stomach and gives you bad news. Hard work is important for all success. But what's even better than hard work is smart work. Smart work is all about leveraging your understanding and improving of your previous actions and methods. It's about leveraging technologies that currently exist. Creating systems or following systems that allow you to get more done in less time so that you can focus on your strengths on the things that you're really good at. I'm a big believer in going all in and focusing on your God given talents and strengths.

Hustle to me also means to be resourceful. This is something you must learn to be successful because it's part of the process. Business and life is never how we plan it, there are detours and obstacles everywhere. Being resourceful is one of the missing ingredients for most young and older entrepreneurs. I often find myself struggling with being resourceful from time to time. A couple things that I personally do for smart hustle, is that I wake up early in the morning, and I try to do the most difficult tasks early in the day so my days are top heavy.

Writing things down the night before helps me hustle smart. I also reflect at the end of that day to see what went well, and how could I improve. Leveraging technology is one of the best ways to hustle smart. From using platforms like YouTube, Facebook, Instagram to leverage your message. Video is the most powerful way to do this from my opinion. Creating online funnels that collect leads, nurture clients and sell products online is one of the ways business has changed over the last 10 years. So work hard and then focus on turning that hard work into smart hustle.

U is for Uncomfortable. You must get comfortable with being uncomfortable. Getting in front of a large audience makes some people uncomfortable but can allow you to grow personally and in your business. Making tough decisions is never easy. When you have to fire an employee because they are not an asset to your company, they are now a liability is never easy. It's like a muscle. Now, keep in mind, everybody has fear. There's not one person in this world that doesn't fear something. But not everyone moves past their fears. Get uncomfortable, grow, stretch yourself. If you are willing to do the things that scares you on the other side of that are incredible blessings that life can give you. Not only that, this will build incredible confidence that will allow you to do greater things. Get uncomfortable as much as you can, and there's different layers of uncomfortableness. But this will make you feel invincible!

S is for Student. Being a great student is super important. I'm not talking about your traditional student in school. I'm talking about being extremely curious in your craft. I consider myself a student of life. I am always learning, I am always curious, and I'm always asking questions. The better your questions, the more detailed, the better the answer. Find mentors who can help you with your thirst for knowledge. I love to ask question to others but sometimes over looked are the questions we ask ourselves. Tony Robins once said "The quality of your life is and a direct reflection of the quality of questions you ask yourself" For example.. Instead of asking yourself, "Why can I not afford this house?" Ask yourself, "What do I need to do to afford this house?" Those are both questions, a very different quality types of questions.

L is for Leadership. Leadership is something that cannot be overlooked. Leadership starts with the man in the mirror. Your job is to sell the vision, first and foremost to yourself, but also to your team. You are the visionary of your company or for your purpose. You have to believe.. so the most important person you can lead is yourself. Lead by example. You have to be in the trenches, and do the things that you tell other people to do. Especially with parenting. Kids are very interesting, because they see what you do more than what they hear you say. If I tell my son, "Don't say bad words," but he see me cuss nonstop then that negates what he hears. It's not what you say, but it's what you do. Leadership is critical for becoming the better you.

E is for Energy. Physical Energy is what moves your body to get things done. I personally love coffee in the morning. But truth be told, I don't think that' real pure energy. I think the pure energy comes from healthier sources. I believe to increase your energy levels, you must exercise on a daily basis. If you're not used to exercising a lot, then just start with five minutes a day. My life is always better when I'm exercising daily. Now keep in mind, I don't exercise every day. But when I do, my life is absolutely incredible.

Stay physical. I like to walk in the morning, I like to jump rope, I like to do rebounding, I like to skateboard, I like to ride my bike, I love to play baseball. Those are just some fun activities that allow me to move and sweat. I feel better when I don't eat a lot of meat, when I don't eat a lot of bread, when I don't eat a lot of oily foods. It's also a good idea to avoid sodas and sugars. When I focus on being healthy, life is just so much better. All of this will help you with your mindset.

C is for consistency. This is the key to all success. No matter what goal you have, whether you want to get fit, whether you want to stop smoking, whether you want to grow your business, whether you want to become the best you, consistency is the absolute key. If I want to stop smoking, and I'm not consistent about making that decision to not smoke, I'll never stop smoking. If I want to get in shape and I'm not consistently going to the gym and eating healthier, I will never get in shape. If I want to have a successful business but I don't consistently create content, or consistently get in front of the right people, and close people on a consistent level, I will not achieve that result. Consistency is the key to everything you want. What are you being consistent at?

O is to be Original. Be yourself. You don't need to be the next Gary Vee, you don't need to be the next Grant Cardone, you don't need to be the next Tai Lopez. All you need to do is be you. You do you. One of the biggest challenges that I personally face, is that I don't fully express myself because of my 8 year old son. I'm a real person with colorful language, and real emotions, and sometimes they're raw from my perspective. I often find myself censoring myself. That feels like it suffocates my spirit, if I'm not just raw and real. I feel like I'm not fully living to my potential. This is something that I'm personally faced with. Be yourself, be original. Deep down inside, you know if you're being real with yourself.

D is for Delegate. Delegation, this is a skillset that you either have to learn, or you will be limited with success. The bigger the dream, the bigger the team.. Delegation for me, was very painful to learn. For many, many years I did it wrong, and I'm finally getting the better grasp at it. I used to delegate by just giving somebody the work load, and telling them what I expected, what I wanted, and, "I'll see you in about a month." But that's equivalent to just dumping workload to an employee. Let's pretend you want to build a bridge, and you hire a company. It's a million dollars, and it needs to be built in five months. "Here you go, here's the money, I'll see you in five months." That's how I personally used to delegate.

What happens is that when you come back five months later, that bridge is crooked, you're over budget, it's not even finished, and people are getting hurt on the job site. That's how I used to delegate. But now, instead of just kind of handing off a project to somebody, you have to give them feedback, you have to give them the tools and resources, you have to give them expectations. You have to give them timelines, and you have to check up on these timelines to make sure everything's right. You let them do the process, but be there just in case you need to make any corrections. Be there as support. Delegation is a game changer!

E is for Ethics. At the end of the day, you have to look in the mirror. You have to like who you are. It's not worth quick financial gains if your foundation is not strong with great, ethical values. This doesn't mean you didn't make mistakes in the past, and it doesn't mean you can't correct them. That's part of being ethical, is correcting your past. That's something that is important. I always make attempts to correct my past with many people, just for me, and for closure for them as well.

Ethics is really important. This is something that I believe is taught at a young age, and your values from your parents, and what if your parents didn't give you great values. If you're aware of it, then you can change them. If you're not aware of it, then you cannot change. You need to be able to look in a mirror, and like what you see. If you don't like what you see, ask yourself the hard questions, "Why do I not like what I see?"

That's what the HUSTLE CODE means to me. Now, the reason these things are important, it's because everybody has big dreams, everybody has big visions, but you have to learn from people who have not only been there, but also fallen from grace. People who had to relearn these lessons over and over again. Nobody's prefect, and I know sometimes the journey is very lonely, very difficult, and sometimes it seems bleak.

But if you don't give up, you keep moving towards them, everything's going to be alright. I want to wish you the very best, and even if you don't know who I am, or I don't know who you are, I just want you to know that I'm rooting for you. I want you to become successful, I want you to give back to your community, I want you to leave a legacy for your children. I want the absolute best for you, and just don't give up. You keep moving forward, and I'll see you at the top.

Marcos Orozco is a speaker, best selling author and founder of Gentepreneur.com and BookFamous.com. He is an influential thought leader for the Latino Success Movement which is the fastest growing movement in the United States. An immigrant born in Nicaragua, his parents brought him and his sister to Los Angeles in the early 80's for a chance for a brighter future. Successfully launching ventures for over a decade, claims that the secret to his success is in his failures. Marcos has studied some of the most successful and influential business leaders in the Western Hemisphere. But it wasn't a cake walk for him.. He didn't do great in school and battled addictions and depression as a teenager.. Claims to have been fired from 99% of his jobs and still makes mistakes on a daily basis.. "Luckily, I never gave up. In the game of life, it's not how you start, but how you finish." Marcos dedicates most of his time to his son, his community and lives with passion and purpose.

Made in the USA
Columbia, SC
05 September 2019